Australian Film

GW00383900

www.pocketessentials.com

Australian Film

Saskia Vanderbent

www.pocketessentials.com

First published in 2006 by Pocket Essentials

P.O.Box 394, Harpenden, Herts, AL5 1XJ

www.pocketessentials.com

A CIP catalogue record for this book is available from the British Library.

ISBN 10: 1 904048 58 7

ISBN 13: 978 1 904048 58 9

2 4 6 8 10 9 7 5 3 1

Typeset by Avocet Typeset, Chilton, Aylesbury, Bucks

Printed and bound in Great Britain by Cox & Wyman, Reading

Acknowledgements

I would like to acknowledge the support and encouragement by the following people: for giving me the opportunity, Jerry Raine, my favourite crime writer, and Ion Mills; for careful editing, my father, Derk Vanderbent; for historical film recommendations and Ned Kelly anecdotes, my Grandmother, Nancy Pumpa; for support and encouragement from the industry, Judith Arthy and Simon Hooper; for support and comments, Brady Yauch; for keeping me mercifully fed, my mother, Julie Vanderbent; and last but not least, I'd like to thank the video store guy, Stephen Barnes, for lending his recommendations and expertise.

Contents

CONTENTS

Introduction:
The Founders of the Silent Era

A lonely island continent floats in the middle of the Pacific, apparently populated by convicts and a few native tribes. Who would have guessed that they were a colony of revolutionary *artistes* who had invented the feature film? They made sixteen of the buggers, in fact, before anyone else had cottoned on to the idea. *The Story of the Kelly Gang* was the first in 1906. It was also first in the world to be censored; banned in Kelly's home state of Victoria.

These grand beginnings have landed the Australia of today with a small but successful industry, which often goes unnoticed in the wider world. Yet is has a history of world firsts; in technology, ideas, innovations, screenplays, and political and social change. It has given birth to many of the world's film stars, directors and crews, most of whom were and still are being exported to Hollywood. But their beginnings were in Australia and many Aussie battlers have remained at home, continuing to make film after film for their country's enjoyment. Take note of the greats that have made the industry what it is: during different periods of history the same names recur time and again.

The films included here have been selected for their high standards and historical contribution to the canon of Australian Cinema, not only providing great entertainment through the decades but documenting the history of Australia and its people. There's the Little Aussie Battler; the anti-authority figures; the convict pioneers; the great works of literature; the Australian humour that fights against all odds; solidarity; the innovative spirit; the isolation of the landscape and lack of connection between people; the lessons and crimes of the British colonial past and of early Australians against native Australians, women and the poorer classes of the early colony. Through Australian film we can study the history of the continent along with its torments, ideals, hopes and strengths.

1901–1920
World Firsts

Not only was Australia the first country to release a feature film in 1906, it also produced the first feature documentary in 1901. Pioneering stars of this period were director Raymond Longford and his partner, the actress, writer and editor Lottie Lyell. Together they set precedents for the forthcoming film industry and their artistry was such that their films are still relevant to audiences one hundred years later.

The Inauguration of the Commonwealth (1901)

Directed by: Joe Perry

Produced by: The Limelight Department

Camera work: Joe Perry and Robert Sandall

Technical reconstruction and script of 'Federation Films': Chris Long, National Film and Sound Archive

Content: The world's first feature documentary was shot in 1901 by the Limelight Department for The Salvation Army, and recorded the inauguration of the Commonwealth and the federation of the Australian states. Beginning with shots of the federation procession making its way down the streets of Sydney, it was shot from multiple cameras set up on platforms at five locations in the city, using wide static shots because there were no zooms or camera movement mechanisms. In order to make them interesting, Joe Perry chose high vantage points on street corners. It is a style of shot still widely used today.

During the federation parade there were many historically interesting participants, among them the British Empire's returned Boer War troops, including contingents from India, Scotland, New Zealand, Britain and, of course, Australia. There were also church leaders, cabinet ministers, premiers, mayors, university leaders and an elaborate, Italian vehicular community float.

As the parade drew to a close, the governor general and the new cabinet ministers were sworn into parliament. This signing of the federation documents ended the colony of Australia and began the Commonwealth of Australia.

Subtext: A record, not only of Australia's new-found independence, but of Australia's old ties to the Empire. In the reconstruction, it is accompanied by period music and early sound recordings.

Background: Produced by the Limelight Department, which was established originally to promote the work of the Salvation Army, its first production was a slide show, three hours long, that was made in 1891. Called *Austral Underworld*, it was produced by William Booth, the founder of The Salvation Army. A moving look at the slums of England and Australia at that time, it showed the unfortunate street children, prostitutes and homeless people and the conditions they were forced to endure.

In 1896 William Booth's son, Herbert, bought the first motion picture projection unit in Australia for the purpose of continuing the work of the Limelight Department. That same year the first piece of film was shot at the Melbourne Derby.

Soldiers of the Cross, the first major production in 1900, was a lecture on Christian martyrs. Following this, film projection was mostly used for government information, propaganda, and advertisements for immigration to the Australian colony. Between the years 1899 – 1902 it was used to film the Boer War in South Africa. The most interesting footage is of the Bicycle Corp: troops who actually rode bikes into battle. Finally, in 1901, the Limelight Department made history with the first documentary, *The Inauguration of the Commonwealth*.

Verdict: The importance of this historical document for the film industry world wide is phenomenal. It is widely known as the first film record of the birth of a nation.

The Story of the Kelly Gang (1906)

Directed by: Charles Tait

Written by: Charles Tait

Assistant Director: Sam Crewes

Cast: Godfrey Cass (Ned Kelly), Nicholas Brierley (Joe Byrne), Elizabeth Tait (Kate Kelly), John Tait (School Master), Bella Cola, Vera Linden, Frank Mills, Ollie Wilson, E.J. Tait (extra), Frank Tait (extra). The film is estimated to have used 6000 feet of film and to have run for between 70 and 80 minutes.

Produced by: W.A.Gibson, Millard Johns, John Tait, Nevin Tait

Cinematography by: Millard Johnson, Orrie Perry, Reg Perry

Story: This fast-paced action film was the first feature film in the world, also the first censored. The film was banned in the state of Victoria where Ned Kelly's family had lived twenty years earlier[1]. Only a few film stills, a story synopsis and some newspaper clippings survive. This true story followed the Irish squatters, the Kelly family and their harassment by the Victorian police.

The final scene is the most memorable. Ned Kelly is shot numerous times by the police but doesn't die. He staggers across the screen until he is captured by the police. He is portrayed as the last of the bushrangers and the first of the masked heroes.

Subtext: The masked bandit inspired a century of Australian crime films, notably *Robbery Under Arms* made twice, first in 1907 and again in 1920 (also see *Ned Kelly*). Kelly was a Robin Hood figure. He stood up to the corrupt police force which was stealing from the poor pioneers of Australia. He stole money from banks and gave it to the poor settlers. He supposedly stole land mortgage papers from the banks and burnt them so that struggling families wouldn't be in debt. He was the first of the legendary Australian bank robbers.

Background: This was the longest film ever made and thus the first feature film: using thousands of feet of film, it was between 70 and 80 minutes long. Produced by the Tait family, it was written by Charles Tait, and famous for its loud, heart-racing gun shots and other sound effects. The cinematographers, Reg and Orrie Perry, were both involved in *Soldiers of the Cross*, which was directed by their father, Joseph Perry in 1900 along with Herbert Booth. *Soldiers of the Cross* was the first film production by the Limelight Department but not a feature film. It was made up of pieces of film separated by coloured slides[2].

Verdict: By the time other countries had begun making feature films in 1911 Australia had already made 16[3]. This was the beginning of film history.

The Mutiny of the Bounty (1916)

Directed by: Raymond Longford

Written by: Raymond Longford, Lottie Lyell

Cast: Gwil Adams (Mrs. Bligh), Mere Amohau (Mere), Harry Beaumont (Mr. Samuels), Reginald Collins (Midshipman Heywood), Ernesto Crosetto (Midshipman Hallett), George Cross (William Bligh), D.L. Dalziel (Sir Joseph Banks), Ada Guilford (Mrs. Heywood), Lottie Lyell (Nessy Heywood), Leah Miller (Baby), Wilton Power (Fletcher Christian) 55 minutes

Produced By: Raymond Longford

Edited by: Lottie Lyell

Cinematography: Franklyn Barrett, Charles Newham, A.O. Segerberg

Story: This is a popular piece of British colonial history and has since been remade into five separate films (three Australian productions and two American).

Captain Bligh and his crew voyage to Tahiti, where they are consigned to pick up a shipment of bread fruit. An excellent seaman, Captain Bligh has a few personality issues which incense his first mate, Fletcher Christian. Coupled with Bligh's personality flaws, is Christian's love of Tahiti and desire to stay, which eventually leads Christian to the mutiny that sets Bligh and his crew adrift in a row boat on the Pacific Ocean. Left with only sufficient food to reach a neighbouring island which is populated by hostile natives, Captain Bligh is forced to navigate 3,618 nautical miles to Timor; 41 days by open row boat.

The History and subtext: Fletcher Christian's mutiny of Captain Bligh's ship, 'The Bounty', in 1789 has had long reaching affects on the history of the British Empire. The ancestors of Fletcher Christian and the mutineers still live on the island of Pitcairn, in the Pacific.

It wasn't the last mutiny that Captain Bligh suffered. In 1805, three years after he was appointed Governor of NSW, the whole colony mutinied and he was finally imprisoned for his cruelty. Despite this he was one of the colony's first powerful pioneers, and a brilliant seaman and navigator. While he has Australia to show for it, Fletcher Christian and his ancestors have a small volcanic rock named Pitcairn with a population of 47 and a history of sexual abuse scandals and Seventh Day Adventist missionaries.

Background: This first Bounty film was a 55 minute, black and white, silent production directed by the well-known Raymond Longford (See *The Sentimental Bloke*), written by himself and his partner Lottie Lyell. Lottie also acted in the film and was Australia's favourite actor and writer of the time.

Verdict: A must see Australian classic, especially for fans of Lottie Lyell (see *The Sentimental Bloke*).

Also worth noting are:

In the Wake of the Bounty (1933)

A 65 minute production written and directed by Charles Chauvel, also famous for the classic groundbreaking films

Jedda, 40,000 horsemen and *The Rats of Tobruk*, among others. The film was an international success mostly due to the controversial Australian star of the time, Errol Flynn, who was later snapped up by Hollywood.

The Bounty (1984)

Based on Richard Hough's book by the same name, this was a success due to its all star cast. Australian success Mel Gibson leads the team as Fletcher Christian and performs some fantastic scenes of madness. The film also stars Anthony Hopkins, Laurence Olivier, Edward Fox, Daniel Day-Lewis, Bernard Hill, Philip Davis and Liam Neeson. It was directed and written by Roger Donaldson and Robert Bolt, respectively.

The Sentimental Bloke (1919)

Directed by: Raymond Longford

Written by: C.J. Dennis (poem), Raymond Longford, Lottie Lyell

Cast: Arthur Tauchert (The Bloke), Lottie Lyell (Doreen), Gilbert Emery (Ginger Mick), Stanley Robinson (The Bloke's Friend), Harry Young (The Stror 'at Coot), Margaret Reid (Mother), Charles Keegan (Parson), William Coulter (Uncle Jim), Helen Fergus (Nurse), C.J. Dennis (Himself) 72 minutes

Produced by: Raymond Longford

Edited by: Lottie Lyell

Cinematography: Arthur Higgins

Assistant Directors: Arthur Cross, Clyde Marsh

Story: Based on the famous poem of the same name, this is a realistic love story about two ordinary people. The bloke (Arthur Tauchert) is a rough sort who is pinched for stoushing some cops when they catch him at an illegal two-up game. He's released after six months and spots a good-looking tart, which in those days meant a good-looking lady. He falls head over heels in love and gets a steady job hawking goods. He's a sentimental bloke in love and nearly busts his gut on the first date: "It wus a bonzer night, the wet sands glistened and the gleamin' moon shone yeller on the sea, all streakin' down." A charming piano accompanies the hopeful mood: "the band was playing some dreamy toon."

The object of his affection is the spritely but coy Doreen (Lottie Lyell). After a few jealous hiccups and drinking slip-ups the bloke settles down into married life and learns to enjoy working hard for his lady love.

Subtext: It is a down to earth look at a love story; note the bloke's sentiment that Romeo is a 'barmy goat' during his critique of Romeo and Juliet.

Background: This is a beautiful example of the work of Lottie Lyell, Australia's first film star. One of the first women to be labelled a genius: she wrote, directed, edited or acted in most of Australia's first films from 1911–1923. Her tragic death in 1925 at the age of 35 left her partner, the famous film director and producer of the time, Raymond Longford, with an almost empty career up until his death in 1959.

Verdict: A classic film worldwide. With its realistic yet charming ambience and poetic flair, it is still relevant to the audiences of today. 5/5

1920s
Pioneers

"As everyone knows, Australians are mostly criminals…"[4] may be a funny quote, but it derives from the convict stereotype that Australians are proud to be lumped with. The very early beginnings of the colony were founded on hard yakka by settlers and convict work teams. These humble beginnings are a source of jovial pride and have permeated Australian art right from the beginning. They weren't all criminals though; the majority were free settlers. Of those who were convicts, most were either wrongly accused or poor Brits that had stolen a loaf of bread to feed their families. At a time when London was suffering from over-crowding, Australia provided a great place to send the undesirables. They became fodder to develop a colony for the Empire.

On Our Selection (1920)

Directed by: Raymond Longford

Written by: Raymond Longford, Lottie Lyell, Steele Rudd (books)

Produced by: E.J. Longford

Cinematographer: Arthur Higgins

Cast: Percy Walsh (Dad), Beatrice Esmond (Mum), Tal Ordell (Dave), Evelyn Johnson (Kate), Arthur Greenaway (Sandy Taylor), Fred Coleman (Dan), Charlotte Beaumont (Sarah), Olga Willard (Nell), Arthur Wilson (Joe) 76 minutes

Story: Steele Rudd's *Dad and Dave* is a slapstick comedy that delivers the sometimes tragic lives of Australia's early pioneers. The film is in fact dedicated to all of the pioneers of Australia. And beneath the funny possum in the bed and the dancing Dave scenes, is a story of hardship and hard work. The squatters, the Rudd Family, go through drought and bush fire, losing everything until they are reduced to begging a bag of flour from a neighbouring farm in order to keep from starving.

Subtext: True to the Australian spirit, the characters keep on smiling and joking and the hard work pays off in the end. The rains finally come and the man who "kept the wolf from the door" by giving the Rudd's a bag of flour, marries the eldest daughter, Kate.

Background: This was yet another successful collaboration between Longford, Lyell and their pioneering cinematographer, Arthur Higgins. Steele Rudd's story was made into a film again in 1932 by director Ken G. Hall and in 1995 by George Whaley (see chapter 7).

The Rudd books themselves are a literary institution in Australia, especially within the author's hometown of Toowoomba, Australia's largest, rural community.

Verdict: While the humour comprises of outdated slapstick gags, it is still a classic Steele Rudd story which conveys the struggles of early Australian settlers. 2.5/5

For the Term of His Natural Life (1927)

Directed by: Norman Dawn

Written by: Marcus Clarke (novel), Norman Dawn

Cast: George Fisher (Rufus Dawe/John Rex), Eva Novak (Sylvia Vickers), Dunstan Webb (Maurice Frere), Jessica Harcourt (Sarah Purfoy), Arthur McLaglen (Gabbett), Katherine Dawn (Mrs. Vickers), Gerald Kay Souper (Major Vickers), Marion Marcus Clarke (Lady Devine), Arthur Tauchert (Warden Troke), Beryl Gow (Sylvia Vickers as child) Compton Coutts (Reverend Meekin) Mayne Lynton (Reverend North), Carlton Stuart (Commandant Burgess), William O'Hanlon (The Crow) Arthur Greenaway (Lord Bellasis) 101 minutes

Edited by: Katherine and Norman Dawn, Mona Donaldson

Cinematography: Bert Croos, Len Roos, John William Trerise

Story: Wrongly accused Rufus Dawes (George Fisher) is sentenced for the term of his natural life to the colony of Australia. Set in 1827 and filmed in 1927, it gives a historical look at the suffering of the convicts. Some of them escaped and were reduced to cannibalism to survive. Others were merely children. Many were innocent.

Dawes escapes imprisonment at one point but returns in order to rescue a young girl, Sylvia, who was left in an abandoned settlement. Sylvia falls in love with good Mr Dawes but loses her memory. She is then coerced into marrying the evil British Commandant while Dawes rots in prison. Of course, her memory finally returns and all evils are righted.

Subtext: The convicts are portrayed as brave men. They were pioneers of Australia. They had noble ideals and struggled to build the early Australian settlements in a rugged and alien landscape whilst living amongst social injustices.

Background: This was one of the first attempts at sub-plotting within a film. The result appears to be three or four films spliced and then glued back together. For this reason, it feels a lot longer than it is, also because of the lack of sound: it was released just before the sound revolution in film. The American star of the film, Eva Novak, was a famous silent film star, who appeared in some 118 productions during her lifetime.

Raymond Longford was the original director but he was fired by the producers, who gave his job to an American (Dawn) in order to garner more publicity for the film. It worked but it was also the end of Longford and the end of an Australian filmmaking industry for many years to come. Longford's opinion was, "I don't blame the Americans… they do merely what we ask them…"[5]

Verdict: Important historically as the first big budget Australian film. 4/5

1930s
Talkies

Australia had one of the highest rates of picture-goers in the world at this time. Workers could afford to go to the cinema because Australia was one of the few countries to have a minimum wage, but the audience watched mainly American films and were Hollywood's biggest customer.

The picture houses eventually put the Australian directors and producers out of business. Hollywood studios block booked the cinemas, forcing the cinemas to distribute a lot of bad films in order to receive the blockbusters. Australian pictures were squeezed out of the market.

Raymond Longford's career was finished by the American market when he was fired from *For the Term of His Natural Life*. Beaumont Smith, who directed the 1920 version of *The Man from Snowy River*, commented: "Rewards for Australian films are harder to come by and are not commensurate with the expenses involved."[6]

With the advent of talkies Australia had no hope of keeping up and it was years before the right technology was perfected to compete in the talking picture industry. Frank Thring, the first talkie producer, and Cinesound, another Australian talking picture production company, tried to keep Australia in the race, and although a few films were made in the 1930s, Hollywood's block booking was doing a lot of damage. Eventually the government passed a quota law that 20 Australian films must be shown in cinemas per year. The law

was not enforced and the quota act failed. Frank Thring died
and so did the Australian film industry[7]. Though some films
were still made the majority were produced by America and
Britain. The industry did not begin to recover until the 1970s
when the audiences demanded independent and alternative
films to the Hollywood norm. This was aided by government
tax incentives for filmmakers and the introduction of a non-
commercial television station, SBS.

Strike Me Lucky (1934)

Directed by: Ken G.Hall

Written by: George Parker, Victor Roberts

Produced by: Ken G.Hall

Cinematography: George Heath, Frank Hurley

Cast: Roy Rene (Mo), Yvonne Barnard (Kate), Lorraine
Smith (Margot Burnett), John D'Arcy (Larry), McCormack,
Eric Masters (Al Baloney), Alex McKinnon (Donald), Dan
Agar (Maj. Burnett), Pamela Bevan (Miriam Burnett), Molly
Raynor (Bates) 87 minutes

Story: *Strike Me Lucky* is a musical comedy. Mo (Roy Rene)
is a caricature of Jewishness; however, this is tempered by his
Aussie ideals as a hardworking, always cheeky battler. Mo helps
and is helped by a little girl who is being chased by kidnap-
pers.

Subtext: Pre-war anti-Jewish sentiment is the distasteful
subtext of this film.

Background: Ken Hall was one of Australia's great

pioneering directors and this was one of Australia's first talking pictures. Australian film suffered even further after the invention of the talking picture with America taking an even bigger bite out of the market. It has been monopolising the distribution companies and theatres ever since, although many fantastic changes have been made more recently.

Verdict: A funny but slightly disturbing film. 2/5

1940s
War Time and Nationalism

On the 1940s up side, Australia won its first Academy Award®: for the 1942 war documentary, *The Kokoda Frontline*. This began a long history of realism in Australian cinema, something which the nation is proud of. The director, Damian Parer, died filming troops in battle.

After the war there was a rise in nationalistic feeling. Films about the war effort, troops and patriotic ideals were applauded by the nation.

It set the standard for Australian cinema. From this decade onwards the pandering to Hollywood was always tempered by an Aussie flavour of "tell it how it is".

Walkabout and Tjurunga
(1940, 1942, 1946, 1974)

Directed by: Charles Mountford

Written by: Charles Mountford

Cast: Charles Mountford

Story: Between the years 1940 and 1942, Charles Mountford set off on an expedition through the centre of Australia. He was lead by an aboriginal tribe and he filmed one of the simplest and best documentaries of indigenous Australians.

The film was edited into two films in 1946. They were called *Walkabout* and *Tjurunga*.

Mountford travelled 1000 miles. Among other things he documented how to catch and cook a kangaroo, look for honey ants and witchetty grubs and how to make aboriginal chewing tobacco.

Subtext: The journey Mountford took is one that aboriginals continue all their lives. It is called Walkabout. He was explicit in mentioning that he could never have survived the journey without the full cooperation and support of the aboriginals.

Background: An important aboriginal belief is that after a person has died, images should not be shown of that person. As a result many of the people were edited out of the film in 1974 and one documentary was made of the remaining footage.

Verdict: A very interesting anthropological study. 5/5

40,000 Horseman (1941)

Directed by: Charles Chauvel

Written by: Elsa Chauvel

Edited by: William Shepard

Produced by: Charles Chauvel

Cinematography: George Heath

Cast: Harvey Adams (Von Hausen), Betty Bryant (Juliet Rouget), Chips Rafferty (Jim), Eric Reiman (Von Schiller), Grant Taylor (Red), Pat Twohill (Larry) 100 minutes

Story: This film portrays the assault by Australia's light horse regiment on Turkey during World War One. It was staged on grand sets with gruesome battle scenes, including one of the best horse engagement scenes in the history of cinema.

Subtext: Behind the tragedy of war were torrid romances, mateship and cheeky Australian humour that held up in the face of all odds.

Background: Charles Chauvel was well-known for making stars of his cast. His first big success, *In the Wake of the Bounty*, starred Errol Flynn. This film, *40,000 Horseman*, debuted Chips Rafferty who became Australia's most loyal and dinki di actor. Despite his extensive filmography, Chips Rafferty didn't leave for Hollywood and the big bucks. He spent his life performing indigenous roles, ensuring the success of Australian-themed art for decades. He also formed a production company which fought against Hollywood's monopoly of film distribution. Chauvel went on to make film history (see *The Rats of Tobruk*, *Sons of Matthew* and *Jedda*).

Verdict: One of Australia's biggest international successes of the time. 4/5

The Kokoda Front Line (1942)

Directed by: Damien Parer

Written by: Damien Parer

Produced by: Ken G. Hall

Edited by: Terry Banks

Cinematography: Damien Parer

Cast: Damien Parer (as himself), Peter Bathurst (commentator)

Story: The first Australian film to win an Academy Award®, a documentary about the troops that fought on the front line in PNG against the Japanese during World War Two. It really was the front line because PNG was just one step away from Darwin, Australia, where the Japanese had begun to invade towards the end of the war.

The footage was shot by Damien Parer on location. He was also a commentator in the film.

Subtext: It was aimed at showing the suffering and courage of the soldiers who were fighting the Japanese. It was propaganda, intended to drum up support for the war effort. This footage of soldiers at the Kokoda frontline is of great importance to Australia's history.

Background: Damien Parer, a courageous filmmaker, was killed in 1944 in the Palau Islands while filming the US marines' front line action.

Verdict: After *The Kokoda Front Line*, documentary became the medium of choice in Australian cinema, a way of competing with American output. It showed the real world as opposed to the dramatised stories of Hollywood. Even today the effects of this period of documentary cinema can be seen in modern Australian films, many of which are imbued with realism. 5/5

The Overlanders (1946)

Directed by: Harry Watt

Written by: Harry Watt

Produced by: Michael Balcon, Ralph Smart

Edited by: Inman Hunter

Cinematography: Osmond Borradaile

Cast: Chips Rafferty (Dan McAlpine), John Hayward (Bill Parsons), Daphne Campbell (Mary Parsons), Helen Grieve (Helen Parsons), Jean Blue (Mrs Parsons), John Fernside (Corky), Peter Pagan (Sailor), Frank Ransome (Charlie), Stan Tolhurst (Manager), Clyde Combo (Jacky), Henry Murdoch (Nipper) 90 minutes

Story: In the face of the Japanese invasion of The Northern Territory in World War Two, Drover Dan (Chips Rafferty) organised a massive cattle drive. The Australians were evacuating the territory and his ambition was to not only evacuate, but to drive the herd of cattle across three states. Most of the farmers burned their crops before evacuation to keep them from the hands of the Japanese invaders. Dan refused to slaughter his 1000 head of cattle and inspired other men to go with him on the 2000 mile journey. Along the way he set the precedent for *Crocodile Dundee* when he saved a little blonde girl from a crocodile attack.

Subtext: Australia's fear of invasion from the north was a strong underlying theme. It is one of the few Australian classics that centres on ingrown public fears. This can be looked at in contrast to certain modern Hollywood style films that thrive on fears of racial difference, weapons, war, criminals, wild animals, mutant animals, alien invaders and government conspiracies.

Background: Henry Watts came from a background in war documentaries, so it's no surprise that he came out with this war film of marvellous realism, based on the true incidents of World War Two.

Verdict: Another important historical classic. 4/5

Smithy (1946)

Directed by: Ken Hall

Written by: Max Afford, John Chandler, Ken Hall, Alec Coppel

Produced by: N.P. Pery

Edited by: Terry Banks

Cinematography: George Heath

Cast: Ron Randell (Charles Kingsford Smith), Muriel Steinbeck (Lady Kingsford Smith), John Tate (Charles Ulm), Joy Nichols (Kay Sutton), Nan Taylor (Nan Kingsford Smith), Alec Kellaway (Captain Hancock), John Dease (Sir Hubert Wilkins), Joe Valli (Stringer), Marshall Crosby (Arthur Powell), John Dunne (Harold Kingsford Smith) 118 minutes

Story: A Brisbane-born boy, Charles Kingsford Smith, was the world's greatest aviator. He held more aviation records than any other man, including the England to Australia record. His biggest claim, however, was being the first person to cross the Pacific Ocean by air. It was an 83-hour long navigation feat, and it was this dangerous pioneering career which killed him in 1935 when his plane disappeared near Burma[8].

Subtext: An autobiography of one of Australia's heroes: some would say its bravest pioneer, yet during his lifetime he had to face being called a coward. Australia's hopes were often pinned on Charles when he entered aviation races and if he lost or pulled out of a race, he let down the country.

Charles's patriotism was symbolised poignantly by the naming of his plane "Southern Cross". It's a story about his physical courage as well as inner courage in the face of his tough critics.

Background: An extremely big budget for the time. It was Ken Hall's last film and the end of an era; he was really the only filmmaker that competed consistently against Hollywood during that period of cinema, apart from Charles Chauvel.

Verdict: One of the great early action hero films. 4/5

Eureka Stockade (1949)

Directed by: Harry Watt

Written by: Harry Watt, Walter Greenwood

Produced by: Leslie Norman, Harry Watt

Edited by: Leslie Norman

Cinematography: George Heath

Cast: Chips Rafferty (Peter Lalor), Jane Barrett (Alicia Dunne), Jack Lambert (Commissioner Rede), Peter Illing (Raffaello), Gordon Jackson (Torn Kennedy), Ralph Trumen (Governor Hotham), Sydney Loder (Vern), Peter Finch (Humphrey) 103 minutes

Story: The revolution at the Eureka Stockade was a fight for gold miner's rights. It was a siege by the corrupt Victorian

Police on a group of civilians who had blockaded themselves, refusing to pay miner's taxes and fees to the government without representation.

On an interesting side note Ned Kelly was born the same year as the Eureka Stockade, 1854, and spent his life fighting the same corrupt Victorian Police force that the miners revolted against.

Subtext: The raising of the Southern Cross: this is one of the few Australian films where a flag is a prominent symbol. The Southern Cross flag is minus the Union Jack because it was pre-commonwealth. After the country became a member of the British Commonwealth, Australia adopted a flag, which incorporated the Australian Southern Cross with the Union Jack. This may be one reason why the Australian flag is not used in Australian film as a symbol of patriotism in contrast with American films which often use an American flag to symbolise a patriotic scene. The Australian flag isn't viewed as a patriotic symbol as it is stamped by the British Empire; however, the Southern Cross flag used in this film is completely Australian.

Background: Harry Watt was an important filmmaker for the 1940s. He helped the fight for Australian realism in cinema as opposed to the Hollywood films that were monopolising Hoyts and Greater Union. This was another great role for Aussie Chips Rafferty who was supported by three of the big international stars of the 1940s, Peter Finch, Grant Taylor and Gordon Jackson.

Verdict: This records an important historical event. 4/5

Sons of Matthew (1949)

Directed by: Charles Chauvel

Written by: Charles Chauvel, Elsa Chauvel, Maxwell Dunn, Bernard O'Reilly (books)

Produced by: Charles Chauvel, Elsa Chauvel

Edited by: Terry Banks

Cinematography: Bert Nicholas, Carl Kayser

Cast: Michael Pate (Shane O'Riordan), Ken Wayne (Barney O'Riordan), Tommy Burns (Luke O'Riordan), John Unicomb (Terry O'Riordan), John Ewart (Mickey O'Riordan), Wendy Gibb (Cathy McAllister), John O'Malley (Matthew O'Riordan), Thelma Scott (Jane O'Riordan), Dorothy Alison (Rose O'Riordan [as Dorothy Allison]), Diane Proctor (Mary O'Riordan) 107 minutes

Story: The pioneers of Australia's dense heart brought with them "The dreams of Ireland and the courage of England to help enrich the soil of this, their new land." Or so this film proclaims, action-packed, adventure filled with dangerous stunts as a family treks through Australia. Fed by a dangerous romance, the film's story is dramatic and slightly sentimental.

Subtext: Another film about the struggles and rewards of Australia's pioneers.

Background: For Charles and Elsa Chauvel, and cinematographer Carl Kayser, this was just the beginning. Their greatest production together was to be *Jedda* in 1955, Australia's first colour film.

Verdict: The photography of the bush is magnificent and the stunts, performed by the actors themselves, are hair-raising. 4/5

1950s–60s
Aussie Women

The artistic output of the 1950s and 60s began to register that women deserved more respect in society.

Australia was not an easy place for women as a young country. Women were often left alone to do the steady work on farms and stations. They were isolated for most of their back breaking lives, yet received little recognition that they worked just as hard physically and mentally as the men. The men travelled in packs working as sheep shearers, cattle drovers, cane cutters and doing other seasonal farm work. Men learnt to band together and work as a team. Women learnt to live an isolated life cut off from their husbands by the nature of the work and cut off from community living by the nature of the environment. *Summer of the Seventeenth Doll* (1959) laid open the emotional hardship that women faced when their partners' livelihoods derived from seasonal work.

And then, just as city life was beginning to expand, the men went off to war to face death on the battle field and the women took men's jobs with men's rates of pay. Many of the men came back alive after the war and the women were forced back into menial jobs and, generally speaking, pay cuts of around 75%. There was a feminist backlash. Women wanted equal pay for equal work and they wanted recognition for all the hardship they'd faced. *The Sundowners* portrays the classic Australian character: a hardworking, loyal woman who is destroyed by her husband's gambling, drinking and laziness.

Many women also fought for the marginalised aboriginal people, keeping them as allies in the fight against discrimination. The film *Jedda* was the first to have aboriginal characters playing lead roles. It was about the hardships of an aboriginal woman who is raised by white parents and an isolated white woman who grows attached to the aboriginal community while her husband is away cattle droving.

Poets and authors had always recorded the hardships of Australian girls but the films that came after the 1950s seemed to have extra venom. The sad reality is that contemporary films today are still imbued with the same messages about the isolation of women and the pack mentality of Aussie men. For a powerful example see chapter 9 and the recent award winning-film, *Somersault*. The sad indictment on society is that women are still fighting for equal pay for equal work and equal political representation for equal taxation.

On a side note, the drought of Australian films had continued into the 1950s and 60s. Although films were being made in Australia, and employed Australian crews and supporting actors, the productions were owned by the British or Americans and the principle roles played by them. Think, for instance, of such classics as *A Town Like Alice, On the Beach, Seven Brides for Seven Brothers* and *Smiley*. Depending on opinion, this was due to different factors. Writer, David Williamson and actor Bud Tingwell both attribute it to an attitude of the Australian people who did not believe in their own art when it was up against that of the Americans and British. Furthermore, there was prejudice against people who pursued artistic careers, who were seen as egocentric and fairly worthless. Other directors and producers of the time blame it on the monopolies that distribution companies and production companies such as Fox and Greater Union had on Australian film and television. This was boosted by the government's support of such monopolies and its blatant ignorance of its own filmmakers. It was only through changes in government regulation, for example the law that all Australian television commercials must be made in Australia, that a booming film and television industry was reborn in later decades.[9]

Jedda (1955)

Directed by: Charles Chauvel

Written by: Charles Chauvel, Elsa Chauvel

Produced by: Charles Chauvel

Edited by: Pam Bosworth, Alex Ezard, Jack Gardiner

Cinematography: Carl Kayser

Photography: Eric Porter

Cast: Ngarla Kunoth of the Arunta tribe (Jedda), Robert Tudawali of the Tiwi tribe (Marbuck), Betty Suttor (Sarah McMann), Paul Reynall (Joe), George Simpson-Lyttle (Doug), Tas Fitzer (Peter Wallis), Wason Byers (Felix Romero), Willie Farrar (little Joe), Margaret Dingle (little Jedda) 85 minutes

Story: When Sarah McMann's baby dies, she is like so many white women of that time; isolated on a station with her husband away droving and no doctor for thousands of miles. To help combat her grief and loneliness she befriends the local aboriginal tribe that works on her station and she adopts an aboriginal baby (Jedda) whose mother has died. The baby grows up to be a 'wild' teenager who is drawn back to the culture of her own tribe.

When an escaped prisoner called Marbuck (Robert Tudawali) kidnaps Jedda and tries to take her back to his own tribe, Jedda's father thinks that she has gone walkabout in search of her own culture. However, Joe, Jedda's sweetheart, thinks differently and gives chase. Eventually the police are on their trail as well. They are too late to save her life though as Marbuck is sung to death by his tribe and he takes Jedda with him to that painful death.

Subtext: Jedda (Ngarla Kunoth) is conflicted between her loyalty to her white foster mother and her yearning to experience aboriginal culture.

Background: This was the first Australian colour film as well as the first feature film to have indigenous Australian's playing star roles. It was also the great director Charles Chauvel's last film. He died four years later.

Verdict: This film should be viewed with its historical context in mind. A special note needs to be made for photographer, Eric Porter whose pioneering creativity lead the way for cinematographers such as Gary Hansen (*We of the Never Never*) and Ian Baker (*Japanese Story*, *The Chant of Jimmie Blacksmith*). 5/5

Summer of the Seventeenth Doll (1959)

Directed by: Leslie Norman

Written by: John Dighton, Ray Lawler (play)

Produced by: Cecil F. Ford, Leslie Norman

Edited by: Gordon Hales

Cinematography: Paul Beeson

Cast: Ernest Borgnine (Roo), Anne Baxter (Olive), John Mills (Barney), Angela Lansbury (Pearl), Vincent Ball (Dowd), Ethel Gabriel (Emma), Janette Craig (Bubba), Deryck Barnes (Bluey) 93 minutes, black and white

Story: A couple of seasonal workers return home to their women. It is the 17th time they have been away working on farms and each time they come back they bring their lovers a cupi doll. This time they are back for good as the seasonal work has stopped.

Subtext: This film explores the anger and tension involved in relationships when the man is out of work. Issues of self esteem and commitment are suddenly brought to the forefront as emotions explode. As this film was shot in 1959, it is one of the first films to explicitly question the practicality of the stereotypical working roles of the male and female within a relationship. It explores the man's pride and the woman's idealism, and how those two things destroy their love for one another. Olive says to her lover Roo, "I want what I had before. You give it back to me. Give me back what you have taken." She is speaking of the illusion of love she had when he was far away, working hard to come back to her in the off-season.

Background: The film is shot like a stage production, largely due to being based on the classic play of the same name.

Verdict: A classic film of the 1950s full of anger and high emotion. The acting and situations were so realistic that they were frightening. 3.5/5

The Sundowners (1960)

Directed by: Fred Zinnemann

Written by: Isobel Lennart

Produced by: Gerry Blatner

Edited by: Jack Harris

Cinematography: Jack Hildyard

Cast: Deborah Kerr (Ida Carmody), Robert Mitchum (Paddy Carmody), Peter Ustinov (Rupert Venneker), Glynis Johns (Mrs Firth), Dina Merrill (Jean Halstead), Chips Rafferty (Quinlan), Michael Anderson Jr. (Sean Carmody) 107 minutes, colour

Story: Set in the 1920s, a loyal hard working wife, Ida, wants to save money to buy a farm. The problem is her husband, Paddy, who has always been a Sundowner (a homeless man who sleeps wherever the sun goes down). Paddy has no problem earning money: He is a 'gun' shearer, owns a beautiful prize-winning race horse, has a man who helps him drive sheep without wages, just for the pleasure of his company, a son who works hard as a tar boy and is a successful jockey in his spare time, a wife with a job as a cook and he even manages at one point to win two hundred pounds at two-up.

The problem is that every time his wife saves enough money for a farm Paddy goes to the pub "to get the taste of you and Sean (their son) out of me mouth". Of course Paddy loses their money time and time again, gambling and drinking, and the son's dreams of going to school are never fulfilled. Eventually the wife resigns herself to her husband's short falls and they continue on their cycle of work, drink and gambling.

Subtext: It's amusing that this film is regarded as a classic, touching story of family life. If anything it is ludicrously tragic.

The downtrodden wife, unrealised potential of her son and slacker, alcoholic husband are all portrayed in a light that is a little too cheery and nonchalant. The movie ends with a scene where all the characters burst out laughing as if it is an episode of *The Beverly Hillbillies*.

Background: This screenplay adaptation of John Cleary's novel by Isobel Lennart was nominated for an Academy Award®. The film also received five other nominations including director, picture and for two of the cast; Kerr and Johns.

Verdict: The acting in the film deserves some credit, as was demonstrated by its nominations. Not only that, but the direction is clean and the film showcases the Australian culture, landscape, history and working environment, with some worthwhile shots of sheep droving and bush fires. If you're interested in Australian history take a look but if you're looking for a good yarn, give it a miss. 2/5

They're a Weird Mob (1966)

Directed by: Michael Powell

Written by: John O'Grady as Nino Culotta (novel), Richard Imrie (screenplay)

Produced by: Michael Powell, John Pellatt

Edited by: Gerald Turney-Smith

Cinematography: Arthur Grant

Cast: Walter Chiari (Nino), Chips Rafferty (Harry Kelly), Clare Dunne (Kay Kelly), ED Devereaux (Jo Kennedy), Slim deGrey (Pat), Jeannie Drynan (Betty), John Meillion (Dennis), Carles Little (Jimmy), Dixie (Judith Arthy), Tony Bonner (Lifesaver), Graham Kennedy (as himself) 105 minutes, colour

Story: Nino Culotta arrives by ship in Australia to take a job with his cousin Leonardo as a sports writer. It soon becomes apparent that Leonardo owed many hundreds of pounds to a beautiful woman named Kay. Leonardo has skipped the country and Kay has seized the magazine.

Nino immediately goes to work as a brick layer in order to pay back his cousin's debt. Dressed to the nines in an Italian suit and leather shoes he shows up for work. When he changes into some borrowed working togs he asks the Aussie brick-layer earnestly "How do I look?"

"I don't give a bugger how you look, c'mon!" the bloke says in disbelief. The locals work hard and Nino struggles in the hot sun digging ditches and laying concrete. His hard work wins the respect of the locals and eventually the love of the beautiful Kay. He buys a block of land overlooking Sydney Harbour so that he can build her a house and they marry, after first charming her difficult father.

Subtext: This "Australian comedy sensation of the 60s" changed the way people viewed New Australians. The screen-play poked fun at the Dagos (Italian immigrants): but in a way that endeared them as hard-working people. Nino was keen to become Australian and learn the lingo and work ethic of the native people. The common mistakes that he made were depicted as funny rather than stupid. For instance, when the taxi driver refers to Nino's suburb as 'Kings bloody Cross', Nino continues to refers to it as such. Nobody corrects him because 'bloody' is just part of the Aussie lingo. The racist char-acters in the film are portrayed in a poor light – the police and the drunk on the ferry – whereas those who accepted the hard working New Australian are heroes.

Background: The novel *They're a Weird Mob* by John O'Grady was a huge success in the 60s as was the film. The crew was made up of many immigrants and foreigners. The director was British and the screenplay writer Hungarian. The star, Walter Chiari, is famous in Italy and performed in some 116 productions. The film had a very professional appearance for its time, due to the cinematographer who worked on almost 100 productions before his death and had more than 30 years of experience by the time he worked on this film. The editor, Gerald Turney-Smith, was also very experienced and went on to make the classic *Storm Boy* in 1976.

An interesting appearance is that of Jeannie Drynan (Betty) who made her debut in this film. Now, 40 years later, she is one of Australia's most established female actors, well-known for her roles in *Don's Party*, *Muriel's Wedding* and *Soft Fruit*. Another of the interesting cameos was that of Judith Arthy (Dixie). She later found fame in Britain but has since returned to Australia and has a successful career as a children's author and stage actor.

Verdict: This is a hilarious film which had a profound affect on Australia and its multicultural attitudes. 5/5

1970s–1980s
Isolation by Landscape
Speculative Fiction:
horror, sci-fi, thriller, historical fiction

The 1970s were a reawakening, and the Australian film industry which had begun so strongly was back and better than ever. Audiences were finally calling for originality, independence and alternatives in film. They wanted to see Australia on screen.

What fascinates about a country like Australia is its landscape. It is the largest island in the world, completely isolated with the Pacific on one side and the Indian Ocean on the other. Not only is the country isolated but its populated areas are separated from each other by vast distances of bush, wilderness and desert. This isolation captured the imagination of filmmakers in the 1970s and 80s and lent itself to horror, sci-fi and thriller themes.

We start with *Walkabout* where the horror of children being left to die in the desert is juxtaposed with the beauty of an isolated, untouched wilderness as understood by the aboriginal Australian. Then we move onto *A Picnic at Hanging Rock*: a chilling look at isolation in geography as well as in sexuality. Children in an isolated bush community are sexually abused and then oppressed into remaining silent about the abuse.

We end the 1980s with the film that introduced Nicole Kidman, complete with her original hair, to Hollywood. *Dead*

Calm, one of the most suspenseful Australian thrillers ever made, takes place in the most isolated of locations: a yacht in the Pacific Ocean. But it also deals with the theme of mental isolation that became prevalent in the 1990s, a theme which we will examine in Chapter 7.

And if the supernatural interests you, don't miss out on a young Mel Gibson dressed in black leather as he battles villains, cursed with wearing far too much eyeliner, in *Mad Max*.

A completely different influence on 1970s cinema was the advent of the contraceptive 'pill' which heralded in the sexual revolution. Films such as *Alvin Purple*, *Bazza McKenzie*, *The Great McCarthy* and *Don's Party* were heavily laced with sex scenes, nakedness, outlandish costumes and new concepts of sexual expression. Bruce Beresford was the director of *Bazza McKenzie* and *Don's Party* and he was one of the advocates of government regulation for the protection of Australian Cinema. "People don't watch Australian films," is what distributors would tell him. "Well how many Australian films have you put in the cinema?" he would ask. "None" was their reply.[10]

It was also a decade for expressions by the female sex. Three of the great feminine Australian films came out in the 1970s and 80s: *Caddie*, *My Brilliant Career* and *We of the Never Never*. Finally female characters played lead roles and female writers, producers and directors were given a loud voice. The true stories of three strong characters were screened to audiences: a single mother and barmaid of the 1930s depression era (Caddie), a successful female novelist of the early 1900s (Miles Franklin) and a cattle station owner who was widowed at a young age (Mrs Aeneas Gunn).

"Tony, why would you want to make a film about a woman?" the distributors asked Anthony Buckley when he made *Caddie* in 1976.

Anthony later said, "I thought, 'Is there something wrong with me, or is there something wrong with them?'" The distributors also wanted Faye Dunaway to play the lead but he stuck to his guns and made a star out of Judy Davis. His reasoning; he couldn't see an American actress realistically playing a female, Australian bartender.[11] *Caddie* came out at the same time that Germaine Greer was meeting international success as a feminist. It was so popular that it ran for a year in Sydney cinemas. It was both "commercially and critically" successful.

Walkabout (1971)

Directed by: Nicolas Roeg

Written by: Edward Bond, James Vance Marshall

Produced by: Anthony J. Hope

Edited by: Anthony Gibbs, Alan Pattill

Cinematography: Nicolas Roeg

Cast: Jenny Agutter (Girl), Luc Roeg (White Boy [as Lucien John]), David Gulpilil (Black Boy [as David Gulpilil]) 95 minutes

Story: Two white children are stranded in the Australian desert after their father tries to shoot them before shooting himself. They are finally rescued by an aboriginal boy who falls in love with the young girl and teaches the children how to survive in the outback.

Subtext: The lessons of this story are simple but many. The opposing cultures (Western versus native Australian hunter-gatherer) show us that despite outward appearances, Western civilisation might be the harsher choice of the two. This is illustrated by the lack of respect that hunters with guns and miners with machines have for the land compared to an aborigine with a spear and a boomerang.

Western civilisation has left the white children filled with fear. Instead of worrying first and foremost about finding water or shelter the conversations they have while wandering the desert revolve around not wasting time. The young boy's first worry is that he tore his blazer. The young girl's worry is that she doesn't want people thinking that they are country tramps. Her brother looks around the desert and responds, "What people?".

The children finally shed their leather shoes and embrace the environment. At this point the aboriginal boy offers himself sexually to the white girl but she rejects him and he commits suicide. This symbolic moment illustrates the point that if the white woman can't fill her womb with indigenous Australia, in the literal and metaphoric sense, then indigenous Australia will die out. Without rebirth the aboriginal Australia will cease to be, as symbolised when the children's aboriginal saviour hangs himself because they don't return his love. The white children then return to the harshness of Western civilisation and come to the abrupt realisation that they have made a mistake. The white girl spends her life dreaming of the lost indigenous Australian and the aborginal boy's version of the country that she rejected.

Background: The startling music of four-time Academy Award® winner John Barry brings to the foreground the stark images of the Australian landscape. The people have no names and no voices (dialogue); it is the landscape that speaks the loudest. The main camera operator also worked on *A Clockwork Orange*, which was produced by the same people that made *Walkabout*.[12]

Verdict: While the film is obviously making numerous worthy statements it loses a point for its 'artistic' use of a prepubescent girl as a sex symbol. Why directors often feel that a young girl cannot be the lead character in an 'art house' film, without being naked or without wearing white cottons and a mini skirt, is a mystery. Recent films such as the New Zealand production, *Whale Rider* have proved that young girls are perfectly able to star in classic films without providing such titillation. 4/5

The Adventures of Barry McKenzie (1972)

Directed by: Bruce Beresford

Written by: Bruce Beresford, Barry Humphries

Produced by: Philip Adams

Edited by: John Scott

Cinematography: Donald McAlpine

Cast: Barry Crocker (Bazza McKenzie), Barry Humphries (Edna Everage, Hoot, Dr DeLamphrey), Spike Milligan (landlord), Peter Cook (Dominic), Paul Bertram (Curly) Mary Anne Severne (Lesley), Julie Covington (Blanche) 113 minutes

Story: A comedic look at the relationship between Aussies and their mother country, the land of the "pommy bastards". Bazza (Barry Crocker) inherits $2000 on the condition that he travels to England to further his cultural education. This cultural education includes drinking Fosters at Kangaroo Court (Earl's Court) with his Aussie mates; being fleeced by London Poms for every spare penny and being propositioned by the inbred perversions of the country gentility. He is finally locked up in a mental ward because the Brits cannot understand his lingo: "I need to splash the boots. You know, strain the potatoes. Water the horses. You know, go where the big nobs hang out. Shake hands with the wife's best friend? Drain the dragon? Siphon the python? Ring the rattlesnake? You know, unbutton the mutton? Point Percy at the porcelain?"

Subtext: The Cultural Revolution that Australia has provided England filters through a comedic portrayal of the pilgrimage many young Aussie's make each year to the motherland.

Background: A debut for Australia's 'new wave' director, Bruce Beresford. Beresford is outspoken and his political involvement led to the deluge of Australian films that emerged in the 1970s and 80s, ending the industry drought that had persisted for 30 odd years. His later films included, *Don's Party*, *Breaker Morant* and *The Fringe Dwellers*, and recent international film *Double Jeopardy*.

Three of Australia's great artists were involved in this film: Barry Humphries is a well-known television personality who does impersonations and here introduces his most famous alter ego, Dame Edna Everage; Spike Milligan is a poet, writer and actor; and Australian composer, Peter Best made his film industry debut.

Verdict: A funny story based on experiences that most Aussies have had. 3.5/5

Alvin Purple (1973)

Directed by: Tim Burstall

Written by: Alan Hopgood

Produced by: Alan Finney, Tim Burstall

Edited by: Edward McQueen-Mason

Cinematography: Robin Copping

Cast: Graeme Blundell (Alvin Purple), George Whaley (Dr McBurney), Penne Hackforth-Jones (Dr Liz Sort), Ellie MacLure (Tina), Jacki Weaver (Second Sugar Girl), Alan Finney (Spike Dooley), Dennis Miller (Mr Horwood), Jill Forster (Mrs Horwood) 95 minutes

Story: Alvin Purple has a strange sexual magnetism which makes him irresistible to all women. The poor man is isolated from humanity by his sexuality and cannot achieve a meaningful relationship with anyone. Neither can he hold down a job because he is constantly being coerced into hilarious sexual situations with every woman he meets. Eventually he begins a career as a sex therapist and cures the psychological problems of his patients through sex. When he turns down the advances of his own psychologist she becomes bitter and exposes his sex clinic.

Subtext: This was one of the most popular films of the 1970s because of its unique theme and originality. It was one of the first films to deal with sex in an open and humorous manner and laid the groundwork for films such as *Deuce Bigalow: Male Gigolo*.

Background: The colour, lighting, costuming and set design all lend to the 70s feel of the film.

Verdict: A film that is silly, fun and was unique at the time of its first release. 3/5

Picnic at Hanging Rock (1975)

Directed by: Peter Weir

Written by: Joan Lindsay (novel), Cliff Green (screenplay)

Produced by: A. John Graves, Patricia Lovell, Hal McElroy, Jim McElroy

Edited by: Max Lemon

Cinematography: Russell Boyd

Cast: Rachel Roberts (Mrs. Appleyard), Vivean Gray (Miss McCraw), Helen Morse (Mlle. de Poitiers), Kirsty Child (Miss Lumley), Tony Llewellyn-Jones (Tom [as Anthony Llewellyn-Jones]), Jacki Weaver (Minnie), Frank Gunnell (Mr. Whitehead), Anne-Louise Lambert (Miranda [as Anne Lambert]), Karen Robson (Irma), Jane Vallis (Marion) Christine Schuler (Edith), Margaret Nelson (Sara), Ingrid Mason (Rosamund), Jenny Lovell (Blanche), Janet Murray (Julian) 107 minutes

Story: Set in the year 1900, a group of girls and their teacher go on a picnic at Hanging Rock, an actual place in Victoria, Australia. All of the girls disappear. A young boy has a vision and goes in search of the missing girls. He finds one girl, who has been sexually abused but who seems to be either coerced or frightened into silence. The film ends without obvious resolution.

Subtext: The sexual perversity of human nature, often brought to the forefront in an isolated community, is the film's main theme and also the silence that surrounded sexuality in the Victorian era. It also explores the ability that powerful institutions, such as schools and families, have in silencing victims within that community. Hence the misconception, that the film has no resolution, may be dispelled by the idea that the silence of the young girl is in fact the resolution of the film, which would be in keeping with the behaviour of the time period, had the incident in fact occurred...

Background: ...In fact, the filmmakers claimed that it was based on a true incident of the Victorian era. However, no evidence has been found to support that claim, which only serves to strengthen the film's resolution that the incident was silenced by those who had power in that community.

Verdict: Peter Weir is one of Australia's most famous directors. He managed to film this masterpiece for the small sum of $400 000[13]. It not only set him on the road to making such classics as *Dead Poet's Society*, *The Truman Show*, *The Year of Living Dangerously* and *Gallipoli*, it also pushed Australian cinema under the spotlight on the world stage. 4/5

Sunday Too Far Away (1975)

Directed by: Ken Hanman

Written by: John Dingwell

Produced by: Gil Brealey, Matt Carroll

Edited by: Rod Adamson

Cinematography: Geoff Burton

Cast: Jack Thompson (Foley), Max Cullen (King), Robert Bruning (Tom), Jerry Thomas (Basher), Peter Cummins (Arthur Black), John Ewart (Ugly), Sean Scully (Beresford), Reg Lye (Old Garth) 90 minutes

Story: Ever wondered about the machoism of Australian men? Take a look at this film: a classic tale of sheep shearers, isolated on a property out west with no decent food, not enough women and bloody hard yakka. As they say, "Friday night too tired... Saturday night too drunk... Sunday too far away..."

The film documents the day to day working of a sheep shearing shed which has been one of Australia's biggest sources of wealth during its short history. It also documents the anti-authoritarian movement of the 1950s and the sheep shearers' strike in 1956.

Subtext: Aussie mateship in all its glory. The men work together yet there is rivalry: who will be the 'gun' (fastest) shearer. Everyone is expected to work hard and try hard to be the 'gun' shearer, yet they are not allowed to try to be better than their mates. It's the men's dichotomous art of working hard yet with the relaxed, "she'll be right" attitude that they are famous for.

Verdict: While not exceptional in its sound quality or cinematography, this film is necessary to the documentation of Australian history and gives a simple look at Aussie shearers and their work. 2.5/5

The Great McCarthy (1975)

Directed by: David Baker

Written by: John Romeril, Barry Oakley (novel)

Produced by: Richard Brennan, David Baker

Edited by: John Scott

Cinematography: Bruce McNaughton

Cast: John Jarratt (McCarthy), Judy Morris (Miss Russell), Sandra McGregor (Vera), Barry Humphries (Col Ball-Miller) 106 minutes

Story: McCarthy is a small-town boy who is abducted by a major Australian Rules team and taken to Melbourne. He finds fame, success and love (with more than one girl). Before long everyone is trying to buy him and he loses his integrity. Luckily, love for an honest woman wins in the end.

Subtext: This is a light-hearted comedy with some feminist undertones. McCarthy's downfall comes when he chooses lust and greed over his love for a woman who is smarter and older than himself. The woman is an academic feminist but embraces his football life with an open mind. He abandons her for a rich socialite and his life begins to go wrong. He finds meaning and integrity when he wins back his true love.

Background: Nominated for one AFI Award, the film still suffered at the box office. It was competing that same year with classics such as *Sunday Too Far Away* and *Picnic at Hanging Rock*. David Baker was a slightly mad but innovative director. For one of the best feminist short films ever shot, see his *Squeakers Mate*.

Verdict: An all-star cast gives this film credibility and believability. It contains some great comedy moments. 4/5

Caddie (1976)

Directed by: Donald Crombie

Written by: Caddie Marsh, Joan Long

Produced by: Anthony Buckley

Edited by: Tim Wellburn

Cinematography: Peter James

Cast: Helen Morse (Caddie Marsh), Takis Emmanuel (Peter), Jack Thompson (Ted), Jacki Weaver (Josie), Melissa Jaffer (Leslie), Ron Blanchard (Bill), Drew Forsythe (Sonny), Kirrily Nolan (Esther), Lynette Curran (Maudie), June Salter (Mrs. Marks), John Ewart (Paddy Reilly) 100 minutes

Story: It is the 1920s when Caddie is forced to move out of her home so that her husband can have sexual relations with her best friend. When her husband refuses to give her a divorce, Caddie cannot remarry or even move in with the Greek immigrant she falls in love with because her husband will use it as grounds to take away her children.

Caddie has no typing skills but luckily she possesses a pretty face so she is able to find a job as a barmaid. The living conditions are terrible and she becomes malnourished while her daughter almost dies of diphtheria. During the depression she is forced to put her children into foster care and work as an illegal two-up bookie to pay for food and rent.

Despite the opinion that "barmaids generally have a bad name", Caddie maintains that "most of them are decent, hard-working women, and there are plenty like me who slaved to keep their children". Caddie is known for having class despite her poverty stricken circumstances. People love her for her beauty inside and out. She is nicknamed Caddie because it is short for Cadillac, a machine of class and beauty.

Subtext: The historical context of the 1930s depression and the circumstances of beautiful, hard working women being forced to live in a state of malnourished poverty with their children are clearly stated. The blame is placed squarely on the shoulders of philandering men who haven't the decency or honour to support the women they marry or get pregnant, and on the male-dominated society which made it virtually impossible for women to earn a living.

One of Caddie's fellow barmaids is forced to have an illegal abortion when her boyfriend leaves her; "You should have seen her fingernails," Josie describes the abortionist to Caddie. "Did she use an instrument?" Caddie asks in shock…"If you can call a piece of wire an instrument".

Background: Based on the autobiography of Caddie Marsh, a Sydney Barmaid in the 1920s and 30s, this is a historically important film. It won seven awards including two at the San Sebastian film festival for best actress (Helen Morse) and Special Prize of the Jury (Donald Crombie).

Verdict: When Crombie wanted to make the film the producers asked him why on earth he would want to make a film about a woman. The film is a forceful answer to this disturbing question. 5/5

Don's Party (1976)

Directed by: Bruce Beresford

Written by: David Williamson

Produced by: Phillip Adams

Edited by: William Anderson

Cinematography: Donald McAlpine

Cast: Jeannie Drynan (Jeanie Drynan), John Hargreaves (Don

Henderson), Ray Barrett (Mal), Claire Binney (Susan), Pat Bishop (Jenny), Graeme Blundell (Simon), Harold Hopkins (Cooley), Graham Kennedy (Mack), Veronica Lang (Jody), Candy Raymond (Kerry), Kit Taylor (Evan) 90 minutes

Story: Don (John Hargreaves) throws a party for his close friends so that they can watch the election night coverage. At first the friends are content to bait each other with political arguments and mild flirtations but before long the party degenerates into adultery, jealousy and violence.

Subtext: The tension, seediness and debauchery that seethes under the deceptive surface of the working class and middle class Aussie suburbs, is brought out into the open with the help of booze and political debate.

Background: It has an all star cast and crew. David Williamson, arguably Australia's most famous screenwriter, uses his subtle style to capture the realism of the characters. There are no memorable one-liners but the characters, the story and the emotions made a jarring impact.

Verdict: An important film for the recording of Australian culture. 4/5

Storm Boy (1976)

Directed by: Henri Safran

Written by: Colin Thiele (novel), Sonia Borg, Sidney L. Stebel

Produced by: Matt Carroll, Jane Scott

Edited by: Gerald Turney-Smith

Cinematography: Geoff Burton

Cast: Greg Rowe (Storm Boy), Peter Cummins (Tom Kingsley), David Gulpilil (Fingerbone), Judy Dick (Miss Walker) 88 minutes

Story: Colin Thiele is one of Australia's most important children's authors. This story is about a young boy who is brought up on a remote island near Adelaide. His father doesn't want him to be influenced by society and doesn't send him to school. Instead Storm Boy learns about catching fish and caring for animals and nature. He befriends an aboriginal man and together they defend pelicans on a nature reserve from bird hunters.

Subtext: Another film of the 1970s about isolation in the vast Australian landscape, this time the father's personal choice as he turns his back on society and the material desires that come with it. *Storm Boy* investigates the advantages and disadvantages of a community. The advantages are friendship and education, the disadvantages are materialism and disrespect for the environment, including early ecological concerns.

Background: Scott Hicks, the director of *Shine, Snow Falling on Cedars* and *Hearts in Atlantis* got his experience working on *Storm Boy* as a runner. It was cinematographer Geoff Burton's third film after *Sunday Too Far Away* and *The Fourth Wish*. He went on to make such great films as *The Year My Voice Broke, Dead Calm, Bangkok Hilton, Sirens, The Sum of Us, Brilliant Lies* and many others. He definitely made his mark on the 1970s with his penchant for drawn out, tear jerking shots, set against dreary, isolated landscapes and accompanied by melancholy tunes. Some might say this made him the master of using depth of field to extract emotion.

Verdict: It is an Australian classic which is now imbedded in the nation's psyche, namely brought about by being taught in schools throughout the decades. The film is a little sentimental, but well worth a viewing. 3/5

The Chant of Jimmie Blacksmith (1978)

Directed by: Fred Schepisi

Written by: Thomas Keneally (novel), Fred Schepisi

Produced by: Fred Schepisi, Roy Stevens

Edited by: Brian Kavanagh

Cinematography: Ian Baker

Cast: Tommy Lewis (Jimmie Blacksmith), Freddy Reynolds (Mort Blacksmith), Ray Barrett (Farrell), Jack Thompson (Rev. Neville) 120 minutes

Story: Jimmie Blacksmith is a missionary aboriginal. This is because he is half white and Rev. Neville felt that half whites should be brought up in Christian Missions. Jimmie has an identity crisis. He wants to be part of white culture but he is treated as black. He works hard and farmers don't pay him. At one point they don't even feed him or his white, pregnant wife as they are trying to blackmail her into leaving the "black man". Jimmie finally cracks and takes his gruesome revenge on the farmers that have wronged him. He declares war and kills the wives and daughters of white men until he is finally caught and hung.

Subtext: The history of indigenous Australians is bloody and tragic. The double standards that white police and landowners enforced are shown in all their harsh realism. Aboriginal life is not valued and black people are killed, raped, starved and abused with no consequence. However, when Jimmie takes revenge and starts killing white people there is a nation wide outcry and he is hunted down until executed with frightening blood lust. The terrible subtext of the film is that the farmers don't understand why Jimmie is killing their wives and daughters. After starving Jimmie's pregnant wife, refusing to pay him and raping his aboriginal family they are shocked to come home and find their own wives and children dead and deduce that it must be because Jimmie is a "mongrel bastard". His violence was unexpected by the whites who felt it was irrational and came from no provocation or intended purpose, despite the constant hardships and abuse they had forced on him.

Background: The landscape shots of this film were necessary for creating Jimmie's isolated character and frightening atmosphere during the horror sequences. They are thanks to cinematographer Ian Baker who is known for his location films and recently worked on *Japanese Story*, which captures the Australian landscape better than most.

Verdict: A truly horrifying and tragic film, it is historically important for all Australians. 4.5/5

My Brilliant Career (1979)

Directed by: Gillian Armstrong

Written by: Miles Franklin (novel), Eleanor Wit Combe

Produced by: Jane Scott, Margaret Fink

Edited by: Nicholas Beauman

Cinematography by: Donald McAlpine (won Cinematographer of the Year for this film)

Cast: Judy Davis (Sybylla Melvyn), Sam Neill (Harry Beecham), Wendy Hughes (Aunt Helen), Robert Grubb (Frank Hawdon), Max Cullen (Mr. McSwatt), Aileen Britton (Grandma Bossier), Peter Whitford (Uncle Julius), Patricia Kennedy (Aunt Gussie), Alan Hopgood (Father), Julia Blake (Mother), Marion Shad (Gertie), Aaron Wood (Stanley) 100 minutes

Story: Sybylla (Judy Davis) is a "plain, useless and godless" daughter. Her poverty and drought stricken mother and stepfather decide to "sell" her as a servant to help them pay their bills. Luckily she is rescued by and sent to live with her rich grandmother. There it seems everyone conspires to beat the lively spark of intelligence out of Sybylla in order to make her a suitable wife for a rich husband. She is not allowed to be clever or to have a personality but unfortunately she is not beautiful and that is the only value a woman can apparently have. "I'm so ugly and nobody loves me," she laments. Her Aunt comforts her: "Being misunderstood is a trial we must all bear."

One man, Harry Beecham (Sam Neill), falls in love with Sybylla and she with him. The tragic choice she faces is between marrying the man she loves and having a career. She tells Harry that if she became a bush wife who was constantly pregnant and living for her husband's needs, she would forfeit her own career, her ability to live her life and be her own person. In other words she would have to sacrifice herself in order to marry the man she loved, which is what all women had to choose at that time. Whether a woman wanted to be a pianist, a governess or a nurse, it was impossible if she were married.

Subtext: This was one of the few stories to have a female lead that had a personality and wasn't just a one-dimensional character. It had a huge advantage over other stories that had attempted the same goal in that it was written by a woman. Miles Franklin was merely a masculine pseudonym used to help the female author get published in a time when women were not seen as capable of writing a book. The book, *My Brilliant Career* was based on the true account of the author's attempt at becoming a writer in a man's world and was published in 1901 in Edinburgh. The beautiful aspect of the story is that it will never have a resolution. It ends with Sybylla's manuscript being posted to a publisher. However, the story continues into the real world as we read the published copy of her novel, see her immortalised every year with the Miles Franklin Award for literature and see her career become even more brilliant as she is placed on the big screen in all her glory by Gillian Armstrong.

Background: Gillian Armstrong was the first female director since the 1930s. She felt an enormous pressure to succeed as she said, "If *My Brilliant Career* hadn't worked then it would have been, 'women can't do it'". She said everyone was watching to see if she would fall down, there was an extraordinary fuss and people called her and the now famous producer, Jane Scott, lesbians[14]. She didn't fall down; the film was a huge success critically and commercially. It was nominated for 18 major awards, including an Oscar® and a Golden Palm at the Cannes Film Festival. It won nine of those awards including Best Actress and Best Newcomer for Judy Davis at the BAFTA awards and a Special Achievement Award for Gillian Armstrong at the London Critics Film Awards. Armstrong has gone on to make many successful films including *Oscar and Lucinda*, *Little Women*, *Charlotte Grey* and in 2005, *A Colourful Life*.

Verdict: This is without doubt Australia's best film. Miles Franklin is arguably Australia's best classic author. It was a debut for most of the now famous cast and crew. Judy Davis has gone on to become Australia's most well-loved actress. Sam Neil, while no longer the heart throb he was in the 1970s, is still well-loved and has been a part of the large majority of successful Australian films. Donald McAlpine is one of the country's most prolific and artistic cinematographers, and Nicholas Beauman has edited many of Australia's classics. 5/5

Mad Max (1979)

Directed by: George Miller

Written by: George Miller, Byron Kennedy, James McCauseland

Produced by: Byron Kennedy, Bill Miller

Edited by: Cliff Hayes, Tony Paterson

Cinematography: David Eggby

Cast: Mel Gibson (Mad Max Rockatansky), Joanne Samuel (Jessie Rockatansky), Hugh Keays-Byrne (Toecutter), Steve Bisley (Jim Goose, Main Force Patrol Officer), Tim Burns (Johnny the Boy), Roger Ward (Fifi Macaffee) 91 minutes

Story: One of the few sci-fi movies to make it out of Australia, *Mad Max* has gone down in history as the film that exported Mel Gibson to Hollywood. It is a definite "boys and toys" movie centred on a plot of rape and pillage, set in the not too distant future where fuel is scarce and a civil war is fought on the highways between cops and motorcycle gangs. If you like car chases then this film opens with one of the best. If you like Mel Gibson in leather, then you'll enjoy watching him save the day in his souped-up V8. The film is scarily violent and found a large audience amongst young men.

Subtext: The story brings to mind Hunter S. Thompson's comment that the Hells Angels are the outlaws of the present and future[15].

Background: The cinematography in *Mad Max* cannot be faulted. Even cheesy shots of a V8 revving its engine and the keys in the ignition turning are shot and edited well by David Eggby. It was his first film but he has done some 35 excellent productions since. In fact the film propelled most of its crew into successful careers, from the director and producers right down to the costume designer.

Verdict: The blame for much of the bad fashion of the 1980s can be laid at door of *Mad Max*'s costume designer. If you want to see villains wearing red heart sunglasses and sporting bad bleach jobs, be sure to check it out. 3/5

The Man from Snowy River (1982)

Directed by: George Miller

Written by: Cal Cullen, John Dixon

Produced by: Geoff Burrowes, Simon Wincer

Edited by: Adrian Carr

Cinematography: Keith Wagstaff

Cast: Tom Burlinson (Jim Craig), Terence Donovan (Henry Craig), Kirk Douglas (Harrison/Spur), Tommy Dysart

(Mountain Man), Bruce Kerr (Man in Street), David Bradshaw (Banjo Paterson), Sigrid Thornton (Jessica Harrison), Jack Thompson (Clancy), Tony Bonner (Kane), June Jago (Mrs. Bailey), Chris Haywood (Curly), Kristopher Steele (Moss), Gus Mercurio (Frew), Howard Eynon (Short Man), Lorraine Bayly (Rosemary Hu) 102 minutes

Story: *The Man from Snowy River* is a famous epic poem by Banjo Patterson and was first made into a film in 1920 by Beaumont Smith. This 1982 version is much longer and of course has colour and sound, among other things.

Jim Craig goes through the rites of passage in the mountains and in the stock yards in order to become the Man from Snowy River. He must prove his horsemanship, and his superior ability to drive cattle earns him the respect he wouldn't otherwise have as a mere mountain boy.

Subtext: To tame a wild spirit one must be gentle, is the rather outdated theme of this film. It is executed in a somewhat prehistoric yet charming manner. Jim must tame the wild mountains, the wild brumbies and a wild woman as well.

Background: Sigrid Thornton began acting in 1973 and was mostly known for her roles in popular television shows. *The Man from Snowy River* was her first famous film and she has been very popular among Australian audiences since then.

Verdict: The moment when Jim's father dies and screams towards the heavens, "Nooooooo!" is a great mix of drama and comedy for the audience. Essentially this is a classic film with some fantastic acting from Sigrid Thornton, Jack Thompson and American star, Kirk Douglas. 3/5

The Year of Living Dangerously (1982)

Directed by: Peter Weir

Written by: C.J.Koch, Peter Weir, David Williamson

Produced by: Jim McElroy

Edited by: William M. Anderson

Cinematography: Russell Boyd

Cast: Linda Hunt (Billy Kwan), Mel Gibson (Guy Hamilton), Bembol Roco (Kumar), Domingo Landicho (Hortono), Sigourney Weaver (Jill Bryant), Noel Ferrier (Wally O'Sullivan), Michael Murphy (Pete Curtis), Bill Kerr (Colonel Henderson) 117 minutes

Story: Guy Hamilton (Mel Gibson) is a journalist in Indonesia in 1965 during the reign of President Sukarno. He falls in love with a diplomat, Jill Bryant (Sigourney Weaver), who gives him inside information about a communist arms shipment. Guy betrays her trust and uses the information to further his career and satisfy his addiction to drama. He also betrays Billy Kwan (Linda Hamilton) who is his photographer and mentor. When Sukarno betrays his people, it is too much and Billy jumps to his death in an attempt at martyrdom.

Subtext: Billy the photographer has delved into the sordid corruption, abuse and neglect that make up the underbelly of Indonesia. His frustration and despair is voiced by his repeated catch cry, "What then must we do, what then must we do!" taken from Tolstoy. Billy is the soul of the film and his photography is his attempt to control and save the lost souls of those he cares about.

Background: This was made by one of Australia's most competent cast and crews, evidenced by the number of awards it received. Peter Weir won the Golden Palm at Cannes; Linda Hunt won an Oscar®, an AFI, a National Board of Review Award (USA), The New York Film Critics Circle Awards, an LA Film Critics Association Award, and the Boston Society of Film Critics Award for her "gender-bending" performance as Billy. It was nominated for thirteen AFI Awards, it won Best Foreign Film at Spain's Cinema Writer's Circle and it was also nominated for Best Adapted Drama at the Writers Guild of America.

Verdict: Watch it! 5/5

We of the Never Never (1982)

Directed by: Igor Auzins

Written by: Mrs Aeneas Gunn (book), Peter Schreck

Produced by: Phillip Adams, John Murray, Brian Rosen, Greg Tepper

Edited by: Cliff Hayes

Cinematography: Gary Hansen

Cast: Angela Punch McGregor (Jeannie Gunn), Arthur Dignam (Aeneas Gunn), Martin Vaughan (Dan), Lewis Fitz-Gerald (Jack), John Jarratt (Dandy), Tony Barry (Mac), Tommy Lewis (Jackaroo), Donald Blitner (Goggle Eye), Mawuyul Yanthalawuy (Rosie), Cecil Parkee (Cheon), Sibina Willy (Bett Bett), Tex Morton (Landlord), Kim Chiu Kok (Sam Lee), Brian Granrott (Neaves), Danny Adcock (Brown), Jessie Roberts (Nellie) 134 minutes

Story: This is the true autobiography of Jeannie Gunn, the naïve but determined new bride of the station boss. Together with her husband they travel 4000km from Melbourne to their new cattle station in the Northern Territory. She doesn't know much about the bush. For example, she thinks that if she gets lost she'll just "catch a cow and milk it".

The drovers aren't happy about a white woman being brought to the station and some of them quit while the others either shut her out or make an effort to cause her hardship.

Jeannie is marginalised in the culture of white men just as their subjugated aboriginal workforce is. As a result she befriends the indigenous people who camp at the station and learns about their culture.

Her husband soon becomes one of the boys and she asks him why he has turned from her. His answer, "But I have to work with them, it's important." She replies, "But you have to live with me, I thought that was important." Finally he learns not to care what the other men think, just in time to be killed by a fever.

Subtext: A story of people being alienated and marginalised, by both the human and physical environment.

Background: An epic film set in the never never country. This is the land where you'll *never* want to leave or *never* want to come back to depending on whether you love it or hate it. The magnificent wide screen shots and challenging lighting are the work of Gary Hansen who unfortunately died soon after. It was dedicated to him. Eminent composer Peter Best was given a free reign with this score and he set out to give the music "an Australian flavour". He used didgeridoos and basic beats mixed with classical orchestral pieces.

The most artistic scene of the film, and one of the most memorable in Australian cinema, occurs when the new boss is breaking in a brumby on his first day. Here we see a combination of difficult moving camera shots combined with filtered lighting, original heart-pounding music and enthralling performances.

Verdict: As the boss (Arthur Dignam) said in an interview, the film was successful due to "sheer Australianness... a popular story... it's beautiful and it's well acted, what more do you want?" 5/5

Traveling North (1986)

Directed by: Carl Schultz

Written by: David Williamson

Produced by: Ben Gannon

Edited by: Henry Dangar

Cinematography: Julian Penney

Cast: Leo McKern (Frank), Julia Blake (Frances), Henri Szeps (Saul), Graham Kennedy (Freddie), Michele Fawdon (Helen), Diane Craig (Sophie), Andrea Moar (Joan), Drew Forsythe (Martin), John Gregg (Jim), Rob Steele (Syd) 96 minutes

Story: Picture a young priest joining a couple in the bliss of holy matrimony. He comments on how wonderful it is that two retired people can find love "in the autumn of their lives". They retort that the young man better hurry up, "before autumn turns to winter".

Frank (Leo McKern) is an irascible ex-communist who "loves humankind in general but who has been less generous with certain people in particular". These people would be namely his doctor, his late wife, his son and his newly acquired girlfriend/wife, Frances (Julia Blake). Frances and Frank are very much in love. She loves his will to live and will to fight against all odds while he is just happy that she can stand living with him.

Subtext: Not a romantic comedy in the typical sense, it was written by the acclaimed David Williamson (*Gallipoli*) who fed much psychological depth and uniqueness into the characters.

Background: The artistic collaboration on this film is quite something. Graham Kennedy, who plays Freddie, was Australia's King of Television. Many would agree that he pioneered the television and film industry after its drought in the 1950s. He is famous for the first variety show, *In Melbourne Tonight* where he challenged the censorship laws with his swearing, especially his use of the word "fuck" which he disguised as a crow call. Eventually, media baron, Packer, cancelled the show due to the crude language and humour. That didn't stop Kennedy though and he eventually changed Australian film and television which now allows much more freedom than heavily regulated countries such as America.

Kennedy wanted to play a straight role in this film, however from the moment he walks on screen with his white knee high socks and pink and blue Hawaiian shirt, it's difficult to do anything but chuckle. That was his gift to Australia. Worth checking is his hilarious cameo in *They're a Weird Mob*, where a young bloke tells him to "fuck off" and Kennedy is seen to enjoy it immensely. Leo McKern, who has been mentioned before, must not be forgotten, with an acting career that stretched for a good 50 years before his death in 2002; also, Julia Blake, who has been acting in Australian cinema and theatre since the 1960s.

Verdict: A slow beginning but one can't have car chases, leather jumpsuits and action all of the time. 4.5/5

Playing Beatie Bow (1986)

Directed by: Donald Crombie

Written by: Ruth Park (novel), Peter Gawler

Produced by: Jock Blair, Bruce Moir, John Morris

Edited by: Andrew Prowse

Cinematography: Geoffrey Simpson

Cast: Peter Phelps (Judah/Robert), Imogen Annesley (Abigail Kirk), Mouche Phillips (Beatie Bow), Nikki Coghill (Dovey), Moya O'Sullivan (Granny), Don Barker (Samuel), Lyndel Rowe (Kathy), Barbara Stephens (Justine), Damian Janko (Gibbie), Phoebe Salter (Natalie), Su Cruickshank (Madam) Henry Salter (Swanton), Jo England (Doll), Edward Caddick (Legless), Edwin Hodgeman (Sir) 93 minutes

Story: This is a sci-fi film set across two time periods: nineteenth century colonial Sydney and modern day Sydney. Teenager Abigail (Imogen Annesley) is dealing with issues of self-esteem, first love and parental separation when she is thrust into living history. Confused by the filth and degradation of the Sydney slums, she must find her way back to the present time as well as fulfilling her destiny by helping Beatie Bow's family. In the meantime she falls in love with Judah (Peter Phelps) who is unfortunately already betrothed to Dovey (Nikki Coghill). He must marry Dovey as punishment for injuring her and causing her to be lame: and "no one wants a lame wife".

Subtext: It is a history lesson for school children as well as an exploration of certain issues that teenagers face today, as opposed to the different types of issues teenagers would have faced hundreds of years ago.

Background: One of the few science fiction films to come out of Australia, it is based on the children's novel of the same name which has become a classic and is frequently studied in Australian high schools.

Verdict: With poor characterisation, the film does not really do justice to the novel. The blame for this lies with the screenplay rather than the direction or performances; there were some great young actors in this film. It was one of Peter Phelps' first films and a debut for both Imogen Annesley and Mouche Phillips. 2/5

Dead Calm (1989)

Directed by: Phillip Noyce

Written by: Terry Hayes

Produced by: Terry Hayes, George Miller, Doug Mitchell

Edited by: Richard Francis-Bruce

Cinematography: Geoff Burton, Dean Semler

Cast: Nicole Kidman (Rae), Sam Neill (John), Billy Zane (Hughie) 95 minutes

Story: Nicole Kidman was once an unknown actor. After her starring debut in *BMX Bandits* at age 15, the film that introduced her to Hollywood was *Dead Calm*, a brilliant release that fared poorly with critics at the time but which has gone down in history as a classic psychological thriller.

The plot is simple but maintains suspense from beginning to end. Rae (Nicole Kidman) and John (Sam Neill) set sail for the peace of the Pacific after the horrific death of their child. Amidst the picturesque setting of blue horizon, white sail boat, freckled wife and tanned husband comes the controlled insanity of Hughie (Billy Zane). The seemingly innocent young man with his wide grin turns out to be a serial killer who kidnaps Rae on her yacht and leaves her husband, John, adrift on a sinking vessel. Rae must overcome the killer to rescue her husband before he drowns on the sinking ship.

Subtext: It seems like a simple Hitchcockian thriller and is often criticised for its almost humorous 'surprise ending' which was accused of being tacked on to please Hollywood. Yet the ending, while not subtle is definitely final – something lacking in many thrillers of recent times. With the suspense of the film carried along in part by the setting, the Pacific Ocean, as far removed from civilisation as possible, cushions the characters so that no loop-hole or outside help could possibly be available. Rae must overpower the killer on her own.

Background: Although the plot came under fire from critics at the time, with hindsight it did create genuine tension. The screenplay is based on a novel by Charles Williams (1963), which Orson Welles had interest in making into a play.

The director, Phillip Noyce, has gone on to make some great films including *The Quiet American*, *Rabbit-Proof Fence*, *The Bone Collector*, *The Saint*, *Clear and Present Danger*, *Patriot Games* and *Blind Fury*. His main success here was in his casting, for a thriller cannot succeed without the kind of perfect acting that conveys fear at just one notch below hysteria for believability. The performances of the three actors cannot be faulted, but Nicole Kidman is definitely the star. By 1989 she was already an award-winning Australian actress but it wasn't until *Dead Calm* that she was noticed by Tom Cruise who cast her in *Days of Thunder*, and her international career was staged.

Verdict: A genuinely suspenseful thriller with flawless acting, screenplay, direction and cinematography. Even if you don't usually enjoy thrillers, it's well worth a look. 5/5

1980s–mid-1990s
Insanity: Isolation by Society

In the 1980s and 90s society began to question the role of mental institutions and insane asylums, and the art of this period reflected this shift. "Mentally retarded" became a politically incorrect term. People in institutions became better understood and characters in films diversified: the neurotic genius, the megalomaniac, the drug user, the pyromaniac, the depressed, the socially awkward, the different, or the obsessed. Previously institutions of social control or containment, asylums became places of treatment. People who were perceived to be other than the 'norm' were not locked up as frequently for insanity: drugs became the new 'cure'.

The period begins with *Tim*, the film that put Mel Gibson on the road to success. It's a love story between a simple-minded gardener and an older woman, who are frowned upon by society but nevertheless find happiness with each other.

Jack Thompson played his best role in *Breaker Morant*: a heart- wrenching story of "normal men in abnormal situations" during the Boer War.

The first contemporary film to deal with the displaced aboriginal communities of Australia was *The Fringe Dwellers*, which focused on a young girl, Trilby, and her pre-natal and post-natal depression as well as her anger for the hardship of her people. Nadia Tass directed two films during this period dealing with mental isolation, both starring Colin Friels: *Mr Reliable* and *Malcolm*.

The decade finished on a high note with two award-winning films about mental illness, *Cosi* and *Shine*, and gave the world some of the best writers, directors and performers in Australian cinema.

Tim (1979)

Directed by: Michael Pate

Written by: Michael Pate, Coleen McCullough (novel)

Produced by: Geoff Gardiner, Michael Pate

Edited by: David Stiven

Cinematography: Paul Onorato

Cast: Mel Gibson (Tim), Piper Laurie (Mary Horton)

Story: Tim is the archetypal, simple-minded gardener whose appreciation of life teaches much to those around him. His Father tells him nothing of sex, marriage and death because he doesn't think that Tim can understand such concepts. When Tim gets his first solo job working for wealthy widow, Mary Horton, Dad takes Tim out for his first beer. "Did you like that?" he asks his son.

"Yeah," says Tim. "Good, cause it's your shout." A funny scene but underlying it is the sad myth that a man is not a whole man until he can shout another man a beer.

Subtext: Apparently the other thing that would make Tim a man would be a woman. Unfortunately when he falls in love with the much older Mary Horton they are both shunned: she for apparently taking advantage of a simple-minded, innocent man and he for loving an older woman.

Background: Piper Laurie had been acting for 20 years when this role came around. Her most famous role was, of course, in David Lynch's *Twin Peaks*, and she has recently appeared in the excellent American comedy *Eulogy*. For Mel Gibson *Tim* was his springboard to stardom. It won him the Best Actor award at the AFI and attracted the attention of George Miller who cast him in *Mad Max* that same year.

Verdict: The author of the novel, Coleen McCullough, is well-known for her sentimental stories about human nature and the harshness of Australian culture. This is one of her better stories. Although the film is painfully slow and the cinematography leaves a lot to be desired, it should not be missed. Mel Gibson's performance is poignant and the issues raised are thought-provoking. There are also some great one-liners. 3/5

Breaker Morant (1980)

Directed by: Bruce Beresford

Written by: Bruce Beresford, Jonathan Hardy, David Stevens

Produced by: Matt Carroll

Edited by: William Anderson

Cinematography: Donald McAlpine

Production Design: David Copping

Cast: Jack Thompson (Major J.F. Thomas), Bryan Brown (Lt. Peter Handcock), Edward Woodward (Lt. Harry 'Breaker' Morant), John Waters (Capt. Alfred Taylor, Intelligence Officer), Lewis Fitzgerald (Lt. George Witton), Bud Tingwell (Lt. Col. Denny) 104 minutes

Story: Based on a true incident that occurred during the Boer War in 1901, this film takes place when Australian troops were brought to South Africa to form a special contingent of the army called the Bushveldt Carbineers. British troops were being slaughtered by the guerilla warfare of the Dutch troops and they needed the expertise of Australian soldiers to help them fight back.

After following British orders to take no prisoners, three soldiers were court-marshialled on charges of murder. In the face of overwhelming evidence which should have lead to their acquittal, an unfair trial resulted in the death sentence. One of the soldiers, Lt. George Witton, had his sentence reduced to that of penal servitude for life. He later published a book entitled, *Scapegoats of the Empire*, which outlined the reasons for their trial: the Empire needed scapegoats to blame for the atrocities of war and thus give grounds for peace talks with the Boers.

'Breaker' Morant was one of the two soldiers executed the morning after they received the sentencing. He was a poet and left behind him a legacy of work. His last words to fellow soldier, Lt. Peter Handcock, before their execution were: "Well Peter, this is what comes of Empire building." His requested epitaph was Matthew 10:36: "And a man's foes shall be they of his own household." His final words left the biggest impression however: "Shoot straight yer bastards; don't make a mess of it."

Subtext: The Boer War occurred during the same time that Australia gained its independence and was recognised for the first time as a member of the British Commonwealth. There was much tension between the British and Australians at this time. The inference was that Australian troops, or "the colonials", as they were disparagingly referred to during the trial, were the only soldiers who were capable of "such a thing". They were painted by the British as undisciplined boozers and thieves.

While Beresford did not intend to vindicate the behaviour of the soldiers during war he was trying to depict the circumstances in which soldiers were placed: "The tragedy of war is that these horrors are committed by normal men in abnormal situations."

It was an added tragedy that the accused were three exceptional soldiers who, even as they were being put on trial, managed to save the camp where they were held as prisoners from a surprise Boer attack by using their superior fighting skills.

Background: The screenplay was nominated for an Oscar®, won ten AFI Awards and was nominated for another three besides. It won Best Supporting Actor at the Cannes for Jack Thompson's performance, one of the greats in the history of Australian cinema. Bruce Beresford was also nominated at Cannes and the film was nominated at the Golden Globe Awards for Best Foreign Film.

Verdict: A famous cast, Australia's most innovative director of the time, and experienced crew members such as Donald McAlpine gave this worthy true story the expression it deserved. 5/5

Malcolm (1986)

Directed by: Nadia Tass

Written by: David Parker

Produced by: Bryce Menzies, David Parker, Nadia Tass, Timothy White

Edited by: Ken Sallows

Cinematography: David Parker

Cast: Colin Friels (Malcolm), Lindy Davies (Judith), Chris Haywood (Willy), John Hargreaves (Frank), Charles Tingwell (Tramways supervisor) 86 minutes

Story: Malcolm (played by *Water Rats* star, Colin Friels) is a mechanical genius who works for the tram department in Melbourne because he is obsessed with the intricacies of trams. Eventually, however, he is fired for being "socially retarded" and he is forced to take on some roommates to pay for his milk and bread every week. The roommates turn out to be bank robbers and Malcolm becomes intrigued with developing a way to rob a bank using his mechanical toys. The climax of the movie comes when he turns some cigarette bins into remote control bank robbers and steals a fortune, before heading off to Portugal to live the life of a rich outlaw with his newfound criminal friends.

Subtext: This is a classic tale of the idiot savant. Malcolm may not be seen as the brightest person but he understands a lot more about joy and life than those around him. He constantly interferes in the relationship dramas of his housemates by laughing at all of the funny things they say to each other in their arguments. He teaches them to live a simple emotional life and to treat each other more gently, the way Malcolm treats everyone.

The great symbolic moment in the film is when the dummy, that is dressed like Ned Kelly in a wheelchair, rolls down the street shooting blanks at cops while Malcolm escapes with the cash. Ned Kelly is repeatedly held up as the Australian symbol of the fight against authority figures, a general theme in Australian film and in Australian history; the only civil wars in Australia have been between civilians and police when people have fought for their liberties.

Malcolm makes the perfect outlaw. He has been cast out by his employer because of his so-called mental deficiency and can't survive, even as a genius, in his society. When he builds a unique car that can transform into two motorbikes, the police try to arrest him, but he just laughs and escapes (at two miles an hour). His triumph is fooling the police and robbing a bank in order to survive. "It's all crook's money anyway", they decide when they plan to take the cash, the same theory was applied by outlaws such as Ned Kelly and Robin Hood.

Background: This film was based on and dedicated to the deceased brother of the producer/director, Nadia Tass. She and her husband (the cinematographer and co-producer) went into debt in order to make the film because of the special meaning it held for them both. It paid off when it won eight AFI Awards, triumphing over films such as *Crocodile Dundee*, which grossed better in America due, in part, to some disparaging reviews of *Malcolm* by certain American newspapers. All of the crew went on to make several more fantastic films but this, their first, was by far the greatest. The later *Mr Reliable* is also worth watching.

Verdict: Although the photography, at times, is a little dull, the acting, screenplay and overall theme more than make up for the low-budget pitfalls. Well worth it for the humour and the performance of a young Colin Friels. 4/5

The Fringe Dwellers (1986)

Directed by: Bruce Beresford

Written by: Nene Gare (novel), Bruce Beresford, Rhoisin Beresford

Produced by: Sue Milliken

Edited by: Tim Wellburn

Cinematography: Donald McAlpine

Cast: Justine Saunders (Mollie Comeaway), Kristina Nehm (Trilby Comeaway), Bob Maza (Joe Comeaway), Kylie Belling (Noonah Comeaway), Marlene Bell (Hannah), Ernie Dingo (Phil), Bill Sandy (Skippy) 94 minutes

Story: Trilby is an aboriginal teenager who lives in the camps on the edge of town. She faces racism from the whites and separation from the indigenous people because she wants to be different.

She organises her family to save enough money so that they can move to the "white suburbs" and have a proper house with running water, blinds, a stove and their own bedrooms. Then comes the recurring Aussie tragedy of the father who loses the rent money on drink and gambling, sending the family back into poverty.

When Trilby finds herself pregnant she is plunged into depression, knowing that with a child to support she will not be able to raise herself from poverty by moving to the city to find a job. After the child is born she suffers from post-natal depression and drops the baby, killing it. She then leaves her bush town on the next bus heading for the big city.

Subtext: Based on the novel by indigenous Australian, Nene Gare, this was one of the first films to give aboriginal people their own voice in cinema, told from the perspective of a poor community living on the fringes of the white suburbs. The situation of an ambitious indigenous person as having no place in either a white or black community is similar to the theme of *The Chant of Jimmie Blacksmith*.

The tragic choice that Trilby makes between being a mother and wife or being her own person and finding a career are reminiscent of sentiments expressed by the feminist author, Miles Franklin a century earlier (see *My Brilliant Career*).

Background: The film was shot on location in Queensland imbuing it with a realistic atmosphere. One of the most moving aspects of the film was the music score. When the characters sing the aboriginal song *My Brown Skin Baby (They Took Him Away)* it not only refers to the aboriginal history of the stolen generation but also symbolises the inability of young women like Trilby to have children and survive as mothers in a white world.

The film won Best Adapted Screenplay at the AFI Awards and was nominated for seven other awards.

Verdict: An extremely tragic and moving story made even more tragic by the reality on which it is based. The performances are brilliant and there should be more films like this one. 5/5

Mr Reliable (1996)

Directed by: Nadia Tess

Written by: Terry Hayes, Don Catchlove

Produced by: Michael Hamlyn, Terry Hayes, Jim McElroy, Dennis Kiely

Edited by: Peter Carrodus

Cinematography: David Parker

Cast: Colin Friels (Wally Mellish), Susie Porter (Fay), Jacqueline McKenzie (Beryl Muddle), Ken Radley (Mr Morgan), Graham Rouse (Fred), Elaine Cusick (Mrs McIntyre), Jonathan Hardy (Rev McIntyre), Errol O'Neill (Mr Wilson) 112 minutes

Story: This is a true story about Wally Mellish (Colin Friels) who locked himself in his house with his family after being released from jail. He doesn't trust the police force and believes they will send him to prison even as an innocent man. A crowd forms and attacks the police when they wrongfully begin shooting at Wally and his family. The police lay siege to his house just as they have done in so many Australian battles between the people and the law enforcers, the most famous of which are the Eureka stockade and Ned Kelly's last stand against the corrupt Victorian police force of early colonial Australia.

Subtext: In true Aussie spirit, this is a film about the people versus authority. Australia is based on a history of convicts versus prison guards and Australians versus Queen Victoria's police. As a result the Australians have always stood together, to fight the imperial rule of the Empire and to fight the law enforcers that wrongly imprisoned so many convict pioneers of the early colonial days.

Background: Australians are well-known for not putting up with corrupt law-enforcers and it was only through the fighting spirit of the community, that defended the home of Wally Mellish and his family, that they were not shot down in their own home by the police. (For information on Colin Friels and Nadia Tess see *Malcolm*.)

Verdict: As historically important as the Ned Kelly story, this is a must see for all Australians. 5/5

Cosi (1996)

Directed by: Mark Joffe

Written by: Lewis Nowra

Produced by: Richard Brennan, Timothy White

Edited by: Nicolas Beauman

Cinematography: Ellery Ryan

Cast: Ben Mendelsohn (Lewis), Barry Otto (Roy), Toni Collette (Julie), Rachael Griffiths (Lucy), Aden Young (Nick), Colin Friels (Errol) Jacki Weaver (Cherry), Pamela Rabe (Ruth), Paul Chubb (Henry), Colin Hay (Zac), David Wenham (Doug), Tony Llewellyn Jones (Kirner), Kerry Walker (Sandra) 97 minutes

Story: Lewis (Ben Mendelsohn) needs a job so he applies to a mental institution for a position as the director of a theatre production to be performed by the inmates. When a pyromaniac burns down the theatre, the show is cancelled and they are forced to rehearse in secret with the help of the warden (Colin Friels). The patients convince their supervisor that they will be performing a variety show but they have actually been rehearsing *Cosi Fan Tutti*, the Italian Opera. In the end they shock the audience with their skill and enthusiasm. Meanwhile Lewis, his girlfriend, Lucy, and his best mate, Nick, play out the storyline of *Cosi Fan Tutti* in their private lives as they test the fidelity of their lovers.

Subtext: *Cosi Fan Tutti*: an Italian opera about "love, life and everything" is what the mental patients at the local asylum want to perform. Their supervisor thinks they should stick to a variety show because an opera is "beyond them". However, the insane prove that they are more capable at capturing the essence of life and love than those outside the institution.

Background: This was originally a play written by the acclaimed Lewis Nowra who wrote such masterpieces as *The*

Golden Age. The screenplay won an AFI Award and the film was nominated for two other awards.

Verdict: The screenplay is hilarious and the direction colourful but thankfully not greatly dramatic as dramatisation is often a common problem when dealing with themes of insanity. The acting is also realistic, particularly compared to films with similar subject matter, such as *Forrest Gump*, and Barry Otto's interpretation of the overworked mind left Geoffrey Rush's interpretation in *Shine* for dead. There are a few sentimental moments, highly regarded by some American reviewers, but cringe-worthy nonetheless. Overall, it is a down to earth comedy about insanity and the skill of the crew is flawless. 5/5

Shine (1996)

Director: Scott Hicks

Written by: Scott Hicks, Jan Sardi

Produced by: Jane Scott

Edited by: Pip Karmel

Cinematography: Geoffrey Simpson

Cast: Geoffrey Rush (David Helfgott), Armin Mueller-Stahl (Peter), Noah Taylor (David as an adolescent), Sonia Todd (Sylvia), Alex Rafalowicz (David as a child), Nicholas Bell (Ben Rosen) 105 minutes

Story: Based on the true story of David Helfgott, the famous piano player who lived much of his life in a mental institution after a breakdown in his early 20s. David, as an older man, is played by Geoffrey Rush, who won an Academy Award® for the performance. The film was also nominated for seven other Academy Awards® and won nine AFI Awards. The story charts the lead-up to the young David's breakdown and ends with him, as a much older man, being rediscovered and finally launching his international career. David also finds love despite his disabilities and the stigma his wife faced in marrying him.

Subtext: The reasons for the social ostracism of David are arbitrary. Was he locked up because he was mentally ill or was he mentally ill because he was locked-up? Did society push him away because he was different, a genius? The film infers that society doesn't let people stray too far from the norm without punishment.

Another possible reason for his mental breakdown is explored through the abuse by his father, whose treatment of his family was affected by his experiences in concentration camps in World War Two. It's an important theme for Australians for many have grown up in families who migrated to the country after the war destroyed their homes in Europe.

Background: The film's success began with a bidding war at Sundance and then escalated with amazing reviews, culminating finally in its nominations and wins at the Academy Awards® and AFI Awards.

Verdict: The acting is obviously brilliant in this film and although most people watch the film for the performance of Geoffrey Rush, the young Noah Taylor is most impressive; often overlooked due to his limited experience. 4/5

1980s–mid-1990s
Stars Emerge

The sheer amount of stars that became famous in the 1980s and 1990s and then jumped ship for Hollywood was phenomenal. Australia nurtured hundreds of great artists but the distribution was monopolised by America and so the only money to be made was in the form of film grants.

Everyone loves Mel Gibson, Nicole Kidman, Paul Hogan, Russell Crowe and Geoffrey Rush. They are international stars and they are Australian. Directors such as Peter Weir and Baz Luhrmann can also compete on a world scale. The bar was set and Aussies just kept jumping higher.

Production companies began supporting Aussie films with key producers including Jane Scott, George Miller, Chris Noonan, Doug Mitchell and Ken Cameron. Other stars stayed loyal to their homeland, such as Paul Hogan, Claudia Karvan, John Polson and Yahoo Serious.

Gallipoli (1981)

Directed by: Peter Weir

Written by: Peter Weir, David Williamson

Produced by: Patricia Lovell, Robert Stigwood, Francis O'Brien, Ben Gannon, Martin Cooper

Edited by: William Anderson

Cinematography: Russell Boyd

Cast: Mel Gibson (Frank Dunne), Mark Lee (Archy Hamilton), Bill Kerr (Jack), Harold Hopkins (Les McCann), Charles Lathalu Yunipingli (Zac), Ron Graham (Wallace Hamilton), Gerda Nicolson (Rose Hamilton), Robert Grubb (Billy), Tim McKenzie (Barney), David Argue (Snowy) 110 minutes

Story: Thousands of troops from the Australian and New Zealand Army Corp were slaughtered in the trenches and on the beaches of Gallipoli during The Great War. 1915 saw huge numbers of men sent to their death as canon fodder for automatic machine guns while the officers of the British forces "sipped tea on the beach".

The idealism of the young Australian who wanted to save his country from the Germans was rewarded with a useless death on foreign soil. Only a small part of the film is set in Gallipoli though. The first half follows the young men as they go through hell in order to be accepted into the army and do their bit. And then they train like dogs to be ready for war.

The two main characters Frank (Mel Gibson) and Archy (Mark Lee) are champion sprinters, both running the 100m in under 10 seconds. Their athletic prowess gains them a spot in the 5th Light Horse Regiment of The Australian Imperial Army. Frank's job is to sprint between the officer's tents to pass messages when things go terribly wrong. Things do, in fact, go terribly wrong, the officer's watches are set for different times and so men are being sent to their deaths for no good reason. Archy is one of those men and even a man who can run under ten seconds cannot beat the rain of machine gun fire as he and his regiment are ordered out of the trenches. The film ends with one of the best shots in the history of cinema as Archy is shot dead in the chest while sprinting headlong into machine gun fire.

Subtext: The two main factions in Australia at the time of World War One are shown in equal and unbiased light. The men who fight are brave heroes looking after their country while those who don't are cowards. On the other hand, the waste of human life in war is illustrated as well as the uselessness of it.

At one point the men are heading to Perth to try and join the regiment when they come across a wandering swagman. They tell the swagman that they are off to join the war:

"What war?" he asks

"The war against the Germans!" says Archy.

"I knew a German once," the man replies wistfully, "how did it start?"

"I don't know exactly, except that it's the German's fault."

"And the Australians are fighting already?"

"Yeah, in Turkey."

"Turkey? Why's that?"

"Turkey's a German ally."

"Well you learn something every day. Still, can't see what it's got to do with us."

"If we don't stop them there, they could end up here."

"And they're welcome to it," the swagman looks around disapprovingly at the red desert and empty horizon.

Background: Winner of nine AFI Awards and eight SAMMY awards this film deserved every last one. It's a film that celebrates Australia and doesn't pander to the wants of Hollywood: it shows the war and its effect from the point of view of those that paid the price. It received one nomination for a Golden Globe but was otherwise ignored by the American and British Academy Awards®. Of course they couldn't ignore the talent completely. Peter Weir's magnificent direction and Mel Gibson's acting led to their abduction by Hollywood, from where they have never returned.

Verdict: An epic Australian film. Undisputedly one of the best. 5/5

Crocodile Dundee (1986)

Directed by: Peter Faiman

Written by: John Cornell, Paul Hogan, Ken Shadie

Produced by: Jane Scott, John Cornell

Edited by: David Stiven

Cinematography: Russell Boyd

Cast: Paul Hogan (Michael J. Crocodile Dundee), Linda Kozlowski (Sue Charlton), John Meillon (Walter Riley), David Gulpilil (Neville Bell), Ritchie Singer (Con), Maggie Blinco (Ida), Steve Rackman (Donk), Gerry Stilton (Nugget), Terry Gill (Duffy), Peter Turnbull (Trevor), Christine Totos (Rosita), Graham Walker (Angelo) 98 minutes

Story: "That's not a knife, this is a knife." This is a fantastic comedy about an Aussie Crocodile Hunter from the bush who is picked up by a New Yorker and taken back to the city. It follows his travels through the city as he encounters the 'civilised' and proves to them that being 'uncivilised' is what the 'civilised' do best.

Subtext: Dundee has respect for nature, the environment and native Australian culture. Although the movie suggests that humans are the top of the food chain Dundee still has enough respect for the land he lives off. He reminds us that drug dealers, thugs and stuck-up New Yorkers are no match for a man who can kill a crocodile with nothing but his bare hands (and a big knife).

Background: The script by Hogan, Cornell and Shadie was nominated for an Academy Award® and deserved it, coming up with a slather of fresh foreign humour for the American market. In Hogan's opinion it was, "Australia's first proper movie"[16].

Verdict: A top Australian film that made Hogan a household name and convinced hoards of foreign women to backpack around Australia in search of the illusive and possibly imaginary, sexy bushman. 4/5

Young Einstein (1988)

Directed by: Yahoo Serious

Written by: Yahoo Serious, David Roach

Cast: Yahoo Serious (Albert Einstein), Odile Le Clezio (Marie Curie), John Howard (Preston Preston), Peewee Wilson (Mr Einstein), Sue Cruickshank (Mrs Einstein) 91 minutes

Produced by: Ray Beattie, Graham Burke, David Roache, Warwick Ross, Yahoo Serious, Lulu Pinkus

Edited by: David Roach, Amanda Robson, Peter Whitmore, Neil Thumpston

Cinematography: Jeff Darling

Story: Young Einstein lives in Tasmania (the little island at the bottom of Australia) where he invents surfing, rock 'n' roll and how to put bubbles in beer. Unfortunately, the evil Preston Preston steals his formula ($E=MC^2$) and uses it to make an atomic bomb. He ensures that Young Einstein is locked up in a mental asylum. The beautiful and intelligent Marie Curie inspires Albert to escape and he follows her to France where he proves that Preston Preston is trying to blow up the world with an atomic bomb. Albert quickly drains the energy from the bomb with rock 'n' roll music he plays on his electric guitar.

Subtext: There are many themes that make this film perfect for children. It has a strong, intelligent female lead (Marie Curie the physicist) who provides a great role model for young girls. The theme of peace and music versus war and stealing is camouflaged by rock 'n' roll, which makes it seem more cool. It also explores the meaning and interpretations of insanity and how individuals who have talent are often mistaken for being insane.

Background: The central theme of the movie is that rock 'n' roll will spread world peace. The soundtrack went double platinum, and featured legendary rock from artists such as Yahoo Serious, Mental as Anything, The Saints, Paul Kelly and Icehouse. Yahoo Serious wrote, directed, produced, starred in and recorded the music, the first Australian to do so for any film. It was an international box office smash hit. Made on borrowed cameras and from the profits of a sold car the film went on to gross over $100 million.

Verdict: The movie was enormous and widely reviewed. The most common criticism was that the screenplay wasn't factual; but both comedy and a children's film, it's hardly surprising that the physics of $E=MC^2$ are based on surfing, rock 'n' roll and beer. 5/5

Bangkok Hilton (1989)

Directed by: Ken Cameron

Written by: Ken Cameron, Terry Hayes, Tony Morphett

Produced by: Terry Hayes, George Miller, Doug Mitchell, Barbara Gibbs

Edited by: Marcus D'Arcy, Henry Dangar, Louis Innes, Frans Vandenburg

Cinematography: Geoff Burton

Cast: Nicole Kidman (Katrina Stanton), Denholm Elliott (Hal Stanton), Hugo Weaving (Richard Carlisle), Joy Smithers (Mandy Engels), Norman Kaye (George McNair), Jerome Ehlers (Arkie Ragan), Pauline Chan (Warder), Noah Taylor (Billy Engels), Richard Carter (Detective King), Gerda Nicolson (Lady Faulkner), Judy Morris (Catherine Faulkner) 360 minutes

Story: This story became extremely relevant to Australia's history in light of many cases against young Australians in the last year, who face the death penalty in Asia for drug possession.

Bangkok Hilton follows a very similar theme and spans three, two hour film sets. Katrina Stanton (Nicole Kidman) goes to Bangkok in search of her father following her mother's death. During her travels she meets a charming man, Arkie (Jerome Ehlers), who unbeknownst to Katrina, is an international drug dealer. Arkie befriends Katrina to use her as a pack horse for his heroine smuggling. She is arrested by the Thai police and thrown into the notorious 'Bangkok Hilton' one of the worst prisons in the world. Arkie disappears without a trace. The film follows Katrina, her lawyer (Hugo Weaving) and her father (Denholm Elliot) as they try to tangle with Thai law, language and customs. The Thai police know that Katrina has two choices, life imprisonment or the death penalty, depending on whether she will admit guilt. Her father was a prisoner of war in both Singapore and Thailand during World War Two. He knows Katrina has one choice, and that is to escape. But first he has to face the demons of his ugly past.

Subtext: Explicit in its admonishment of the death penalty and the inhumane conditions of Asian prisons and Asian prisoner of war camps, it also deals with the ideals of legal systems and justice.

Background: 1989 was a big year for Nicole Kidman. She was recognised by Hollywood for her role in *Dead Calm* and she won an AFI Award for her performance in *Bangkok Hilton*. It was also the first big role for Hugo Weaving, who was only 29 at the time. He has since won many awards, most notably for his role in *Priscilla Queen of the Desert*. He is now notoriously known as Agent Smith from *The Matrix* films and has recently received fame for his role in the Lord of the Rings series.

Writer and producer Terry Hayes had great success with this film (along with the help of producers Barbara Gibbs, George Miller and Doug Mitchell). Hayes is known for films such as *The Book of Skulls, Payback, Mr Reliable, Dead Calm* and *Mad Max* (2&3). Also, the writer Tony Morphett, a well-known television writer, was involved. Morphett is best known for the hit series *Water Rats*.

Verdict: A superb moral critique of justice and legal systems, and war; Nicole Kidman and Hugo Weaving are compelling to say the least and they carry the screenplay to the height it deserves. 5/5

Romper Stomper (1992)

Directed by: Geoffrey Wright

Written by: Geoffrey Wright

Produced by: Ian Pringle, Daniel Scharf, Phil Jones

Edited by: Bill Murphy

Cinematography: Ron Hagen

Cast: Russell Crowe (Hando), Daniel Pollock (Davey), Jacqueline McKenzie (Gabe), Alex Scott (Martin), Leigh Russell (Sonny Jim), Daniel Wiley (Cackles), James McKenna (Bubs), Eric Mueck (Champ), Frank Magree (Brett), Christopher McLean (Luke), Josephine Keen (Megan), Samantha Bladon (Tracey), Tony Lee (Tiger), John Brumpton (Magoo), Don Bridges (Harold) 94 minutes

Story: The 1980s in Sydney saw the number of immigrants and refugees from Asia soar. This film follows the extreme reaction of a group of young, white neo-Nazis and their violent but useless reactionary behaviour to the loss of their businesses, homes and land to the Asian communities. Hando (Russell Crowe) and Gabe (Jacqueline McKenzie) lead the group on a violent rampage that begins with their attack on a Vietnamese family, who bought their local bar, and ends with the last two gang members killing each other on the beach while Japanese tourists watch on with their cameras clicking.

Subtext: The film explores the causes of racism and violence, twisting the story so that the perpetrators of violence are portrayed as the victims. An interesting subplot involves Gabe taking violent revenge on the father who raped her repeatedly as a child.

Background: It was this film that attracted the attention of Sharon Stone who launched Russell Crowe's award-winning international career (which now includes a few Oscars®).

Verdict: Realism and originality at its best. The atmosphere is so tangible as to almost leave a taste and a smell behind after the credits have rolled. The film pushed Russell Crowe into his international career for good reason; it is an emotional, faultless production that recorded society's specific racist sentiments at the time, and paved the way for films such as *American History X.* 5/5

Strictly Ballroom (1992)

Directed by: Baz Luhrmann

Written by: Baz Luhrmann, Craig Pearce, Andrew Bovell

Produced by: Antoinette Albert, Tristram Miall, Jane Scott

Edited by: Jill Bilcock

Cinematography: Steve Mason

Cast: Paul Mercurio (Scott Hastings), Tara Morice (Fran), Bill Hunter (Barry Fife), Pat Thomson (Shirley Hastings), Gia Carides (Liz Holt), Peter Whitford (Les Kendall), Barry Otto (Doug Hastings), John Hannan (Ken Railings), Sonia Kruger (Tina Sparkle), Kris McQuade (Charm Leachman), Pip Mushin (Wayne Burns), Leonie Page (Vanessa Cronin) 94 minutes

Story: "I don't want to dance other people's steps, I'm bored with it." Scott Hastings, champion ballroom dancer, sets out to shake up the Pan Pacific ballroom dancing competition. His new partner, Fran, a beginner at ballroom dancing, teaches him some Latin steps and they fall in love, despite her controversial background.

Subtext: Fran is an ethnic Australian and her success at the Pan Pacific championships while dancing culturally significant, yet banned dance steps is a win for multi-cultural Australia. Scott's rejection of trying to be a formulaic winner and his goal of trying to be an individual innovator is a typically Australian ideal.

Background: This was Baz Luhrmann's first big hit and paved the way for his subsequent blockbusters, *Romeo and Juliet* and *Moulin Rouge* (see chapter 9).

Verdict: An innovative film on the world stage. Baz Luhrmann has developed new techniques in artistic direction with his use of surrealism, colour, music, wild camera movement and powerful dialogue. 5/5

Reckless Kelly (1993)

Directed by: Yahoo Serious

Written by: Lulu Pinkus, David Roach, Yahoo Serious, Warwick Ross

Produced by: Yahoo Serious, Warwick Ross, Graham Burke, Lulu Pinkus, David Roach, Tim Sanders

Edited by: Lawrence Jordon

Cinematography: Kevin Hayward

Cast: Yahoo Serious (Ned Kelly), Melora Hardin (Robin Banks), Alexei Sayle (Major Wib), Hugo Weaving (Sir John), Kathleen Freeman (Mrs Delance), John Pinette (Sam Delance), Bob Maza (Dan Kelly), Martin Ferrero (Ernie the fan), Anthony Ackroyd (Joe Kelly) 103 minutes

Story: Ned Kelly (Yahoo Serious) is apparently descended from the famous bank robbing family of the 1800s (The Kelly Gang). Ned has inherited from his ancestors; immunity to bullets and a flare for gun slinging.

Subtext: This is a spoof on the history of Ned Kelly who was said to have taken an extraordinary number of bullets without dying (he was eventually caught and hung). Instead of the anti-authoritarian theme of the original Kelly legend where the Australian people fight the law enforcers, Ned Kelly's ancestor is fighting the Japanese businessmen who are trying to buy his beautiful, kangaroo inhabited island (symbolic of Australia). He also heads off to Hollywood at the end of the movie to fight against bad plots, evil producers and cowboy stereotypes.

Background: The film had a larger budget than *Young Einstein* but was not popular in America.

Verdict: Great story with some comedic moments but it falls apart at the end due to terrible plot twists. A fun movie for kids. 2.5/5

Babe (1995)

Directed by: Chris Noonan

Written by: Dick King Smith (novel The Sheep Pig), George Miller, Chris Noonan

Produced by: Catherine Barber, George Miller, Doug Mitchell, Daphne Paris, Bill Miller, Philip Hearnshaw

Edited by: Marcus D'Arcy, Jay Friedkin

Cinematography: Andrew Lesnie

Cast: Christine Cavanaugh (Babe), Miriam Margolyes (Fly), Danny Mann (Ferdinand), Hugo Weaving (Rex), Miriam Flynn (Maa), Russi Taylor (Duchess), Michael Edward Stevens (Horse), Charles Bartlett (cow), Paul Livingston (Rooster), Roscoe Lee Browne (Narrator), James Cromwell (Farmer Arthur Hoggett), Magda Szubanski (Mrs Esme Hoggett) 89 minutes

Story: Babe, the pig, comes to a realisation about his place in the world. When he decides that he doesn't want to grow up to be someone's breakfast, he enlists the help of the other farm animals and decides to become a sheep pig (something akin to a sheep dog).

Subtext: This film teaches children that despite their appearance they can be whatever they put their mind to.

Background: At the time this was the biggest animatronic film ever made and was a great technological feat. Scores of artists, animators, designers and editors worked on the film for many years and it paid off: John Cox won an Academy Award® for Best Visual Effects and his developments were the basis of many films that followed, including *Scooby Doo* and *Pitch Black*.

Verdict: A delightful film that has reserved its place in world history for its animatronics. 3/5

Dad and Dave: On Our Selection (1995)

Directed by: George Waley

Written by: Steele Rudd, Geoffrey Atherdoen, George Waley

Produced by: Jonathan Shteinman, Anthony Buckley, Bruce Davey, Carol Hughes

Edited by: Wayne LeClos

Cinematography: Martin McGrath

Cast: Leo McKern (Dad Rudd), Joan Sutherland (Mother Rudd), Geoffrey Rush (Dave Rudd), Ray Barrett (Dwyer), Barry Otto (J.P. Riley), Nicholas Eadie (Cyril Riley), Noah Taylor (Joe), Robert Menzies (Cranky Jack), Essie Davis (Kate), Celia Ireland (Sarah), David Field (Dan), Murray Bartlett (Sandy Taylor), Pat Bishop (Maude White), John Gaden (Rev McFarlane), Bruce Venables (Petersen) 107 minutes

Story: Dad (Leo McKern), Dave (Geoffrey Rush) and the rest of the family emigrate from England to Australia and select an unwanted piece of property as a government land grant (a selection). They intend to work as hard as Little Aussie Battlers and build a life for themselves where they don't have to rely on an employer for their income.

The villain, J.P. Riley (Barry Otto), is a wealthy land owner and corrupt politician who does shady deals with the mortgage department at the town's bank. The bank kicks people off their farms when they can't repay loan increases and Riley buys up their land to increase his bush empire. Not only that but he floods the market with whatever crop Dad and Dave decide to sell that season, so that they can't make a profit. The people in the town are finally fed up with the evil J.P. Riley so Dad Rudd runs for the next election, and surprise surprise, wins!

Subtext: A historical comedy about the Little Aussie Battler who triumphs over the authority of the aristocratic class, it gives a true feel of the hardships faced by pioneers who worked hard to build Australia for little reward. It explores the explosive relationship between the selectors and the people who already owned land. The selectors applied for land grants from the government for areas of land that others didn't want to buy.

Background: Steele Rudd first published his play by the same name in 1899. He had sold 250,000 copies by 1940, a huge amount for that time in Australia.

This was Geoffrey Rush's first film, after his main debut in Shakespeare's *Twelfth Night* (1987). *Dad and Dave* had started his career in Australia and he has since acquired an unbelievable filmography and an Academy Award®.

Verdict: It is worth watching just for the screen rendition of Steel Rudd's classic. Also, some of the performances are wonderful, particularly Geoffrey Rush who plays the awkward farmer's son, Dave, with perfect realism. 2.5/5

1990s
Sexuality and Australian Cinema

Sydney, Australia, home to the largest population of gay people on the planet, and throwing the largest gay and lesbian Mardi Gras in the world, provides the ideal setting for a culture that redefines sexuality. Ranging from the tough gay, to the sex-obsessed woman, Australian films will often ignore the gender roles that pervade typical Hollywood films.

What makes Australia different when it comes to sexuality? Films of the 1990s may give us some clues. Consider Russell Crow in the 1994 film, *The Sum of Us*. He plays Geoff, a working class, beer-drinking, tough Aussie bloke who goes against international stereotypes that suggest that gay equates with being wanton or a feminine wimp.

Guy Pearce and Hugo Weaving, two of the most individual and well-drawn characters in Australian cinema, are both cabaret dancers in the international blockbuster *The Adventures of Priscilla Queen of the Desert*; further evidence that Australian film often deviates from typical cultural assumptions in asking the audience: what does it mean to be a man, and what if this man dances to ABBA dressed in drag? Elle MacPherson, Portia de Rossi and Kate Fischer play the mostly nude models in *Sirens*, which explores lesbianism, sexual urges, nudity and secular repression of creativity. Such films provided a powerful presence, paving the way for subsequent American productions such as *To Wong Foo*.

Homosexuality isn't the only sexuality that was opened up

in the 1990s. Toni Colette challenged marital traditions in *Muriel's Wedding* while Sara Browne's feminine, sexual discourse dominates the film *Occasional Course Language*: "What's eating you?" "No one, that's just the problem isn't it?". The quote which sums up the female Australian who is masculine in behaviour by the standards of many cultures, yet believable in the context of the Australian lifestyle.

The crowning performances of the 1990s are those of Guy Pearce and Claudia Karvan in *Dating the Enemy*. He plays a man with a woman's consciousness trapped in his body while she plays a woman with a man's consciousness trapped in her body. Yet audiences weren't confused by their transgender performances in the slightest; a sure sign of how much Australian film has aided in the redefinition of gender in cinema.

Sirens (1994)

Directed and Written by*:* John Duigan

Produced by: Justin Ackerman, Hans Brockmann, Micheline Garant, Robert Jones, Sue Milliken, Sarah Radclyffe

Edited by: Humphrey Dixon

Cinematography: Geoff Burton

Cast: Hugh Grant (Anthony Campion), Tara Fitzgerald (Estella Campion), Sam Neill (Norman Lindsay), Elle MacPherson (Sheela), Portia de Rossi (Giddy), Kate Fischer (Pru), Pamela Rabe (Rose Lindsay) 98 minutes

Story: *Sirens* is based on an incident that occurred in the 1930s concerning the Australian artist Norman Lindsay and his work, *The Crucified Venus*, which depicts his wife naked and crucified. Hugh Grant plays the outraged clergyman whose own wife is seduced by Lindsay's nude models.

Subtext: The purpose of *The Crucified Venus* was to place females forward as those who are crucified by the church. The female characters in *Sirens* collectively ask the clergyman, "Why can't we be vicars or priests or popes?" They also inform the clergyman, "It is because we are deafened by the din of our bodies." Norman Lindsay accuses the church of reducing women to the place of second class citizens: "The body was bad for the soul, sex was evil and women, the embodiment of sexuality, were responsible for the downfall of mankind in the Garden of Eden."

The sirens of the film are not temptresses for the men, trapped by their evil feminine bodies but are liberating for the women and their relationships to their own bodies. The priest tries to hold his wife (Estella) back from the eroticism but the sirens of Norman Lindsay prove too strong for the church. Estella's nakedness is only frightening for her when envisaged during church.

Background: Lindsay was controversial but his contribution to Australian art and literature helped to break away from the traditional and develop a unique way of seeing the environment and cultural myths. He opposed the parochial Australian art of the time while still upholding art as the most valuable aspect of society.

The film has been criticised as an art house excuse to see the naked bodies of Elle MacPherson (famous Australian model), Portia De Rossi (Australia's famous lesbian actress) and Kate Fischer (Australian Actress). Pearl Goldman, an original Siren from the 1930s who posed nude for many of the artist's large oil paintings has commented on the portrayal of Lindsay in this film: "We didn't do any running around the grounds naked or naked swimming in lakes." Fittingly enough, Norman Lindsay was often critiqued during his life for indulging in this same bohemian debauchery under the guise of art.

The film secures its place in the Australian canon through its use of setting. The environment is depicted as sensual, animalistic and dangerous.

Verdict: It is a sensual film that has meanness hidden beneath the surface; add to this the somewhat frightening environment and the result is a film that belongs to Australian artistry. 3.5/5

The Adventures of Priscilla Queen of the Desert (1994)

Directed and Written by: Stephen Elliot

Produced by: Al Clarke, Rebel Russell, Michael Hamlyn, Sue Seeary

Edited by: Sue Blainey

Cinematography: Brian Beheny

Cast: Terence Stamp (Ralph/Bernadette), Hugo Weaving (Anthony 'Tick'), Guy Pearce (Adam Whitely/Felicia), Bill Hunter (Bob) 104 minutes

Story: Two drag queens and a transsexual head west from Sydney in a pink bus named Priscilla. Their goal is to reach Alice Springs to perform their cabaret act. Along the way they meet hardened bush types who either welcome them as a breath of fresh air or abuse them for being prancing queens.

Hugo Weaving, well known as Agent Smith from the Matrix and Elrond from Lord of the Rings series, plays a drag queen with a shunned past as a father. He is not only going to Alice Springs to perform a Cabaret act but to meet his son for the first time. The touching acceptance of his son is captured when he asks his father if he will have a boyfriend when they return to Sydney. When Weaving says that he probably will have a boyfriend the son's simple response is, "Good".

Subtext: Such an innocent acceptance of a gay father seems to dispel 40 years of prejudice that a minute earlier had lined the man's face.

Bernadette is another strong character. A feminine transsexual who beats up some would-be rapists and falls for a bushman named Bob because, "he's a gentleman".

Background: Bob the bushman was played by actor Bill Hunter who at the time of filming was also working on *Muriel's Wedding*, another film with sexuality as a core theme.

The third drag queen is of course Guy Pearce; while it may be hard to imagine the star of *Memento*, *L.A. Confidential* and *The Count of Monte Cristo* as gay, as usual he gives a flawless performance and makes even the staunchest sexist laugh at the woman inside all men.

The film was based in part on the life of Sydney based drag queen, Cindy Pastel, whose character is played by Hugo Weaving. Stephen Elliot has written and directed several films since *Priscilla* but none have enjoyed the same level of acclaim.

Verdict: The film was an international success, winning an Academy Award® for its costume, "The thong dress", and bringing to forefront many ideas about gender and sexuality, which continue to have relevance nearly ten years after production. 5/5

The Sum of Us (1994)

Directors: Geoff Burton, Kevin Dowling

Writer: David Stevens (also the play by the same name)

Produced by: Rod Allan, Hal McElroy, Errol Sullivan, Kevin Dowling, Hal Kessler, Donald Scatena

Edited by: Frans Vandenburg

Cinematography: Geoff Burton

Cast: Russell Crowe (Jeff), Jack Thompson (Harry) 100 minutes

Story: Jack Thompson, who has starred in an extraordinary number of films, 64 to be exact, plays Harry, the typical Australian Dad. The star of the show though is his gay son, Jeff. Russell Crowe's gung-ho performance of the gay Aussie bloke pioneered the way for well-rounded gay characters in cinema.

Subtext: *The Sum of Us* explores the relationships between parents and children, examining the extent to which a person's sexuality and ability to receive love in the wider world are inherited from their childhood experiences. As Harry says, "Our children are only the sum of us; what we add up to. Ashamed of Jeff? Never."

"Up your bum" is a typical toast that illustrates Harry's public approach to his son's sexuality. He jokes in an Aussie way about his son being "cheerful" and even offers his son's boyfriend some gay porn in case he needs help getting in the mood. His attitude towards sex is very open; open enough to tease Jeff, also to have a chat with his boyfriends when he brings them home from the pub at night.

Background: Kevin Dowling, popular director of many Hollywood television series such as *The Gilmore Girls*, *Touched by an Angel* and *Judging Amy*, really lifted his game with this landmark Australian classic, with the help of director Geoff Burton, who had worked on over 50 productions as cinematographer. An art film, *The Sum of Us* is not politically correct in the strict sense of the word. Where a Hollywood film of the same era may have used terms such as "poofta" and "dyke" in offensive dialogue, here they are used naturally in a humorous way that removes any offense previously attached to such terms. Harry tells his son, "Your Grandmother once said, 'The greatest explorers are those of the human heart'". And Jeff responds, "Is that why she became a dyke?" It isn't politically correct because it doesn't follow rules, it breaks them.

The film pokes fun at discriminatory themes, such as AIDS being linked to gay sex: Harry, for instance, makes a fool out of himself when he warns one of Jeff's friends to practice safe sex because of AIDS. *Philadelphia*, the American film that came out around the same time treated its subject very differently. With a serious, tear-jerking storyline, it could now be viewed as an agitator for the negative association drawn between gay people and AIDS.

The Sum of Us does have its sentimental moments but they are tempered with humour. For example, when Harry is crippled by a stroke and unable to speak, Jeff now defends him. The stroke hinders their communication and when Jeff falls in love he mistakes his father's tears of joy for those of disappointment, until finally Harry can communicate to his son his happiness using not words but a series of hilarious eye rolls and finger taps.

It won awards at the Cleveland International Film Festival, Montreal Film Festival and the AFI Awards.

Verdict: A combination of realistic acting, down-to-earth characters and a well-balanced screenplay, this movie really opened people's eyes to its subject-matter. 4/5

Muriel's Wedding (1994)

Director and writer: P.J. Hogan

Produced by: Lynda House, Tony Mahood, Jocelyn Moorhouse, Michael Aglion

Edited by: Jil Bilcock

Cinematography by: Martin McGrath

Cast: Sophie Lee (Tania Degano), Toni Collette (Muriel Heslop), Bill Hunter (Bill Heslop), Jeanie Drynan (Betty Heslop), Gennie Nevinson (Deidre Chambers), Rachel Griffiths (Rhonda Epinstalk), Matt Day (Brice Nobes), 106 minutes

Story: Muriel is obsessed with marriage, and believes that if someone will marry her life will suddenly have meaning and she will no longer be useless. As the traditional roles of mother, father and family disintegrate around her, Muriel holds fast to her wedding fantasies. Her only saving grace is a new friend who helps change her life for the better, bringing Muriel out of her deluded dream world and into a reality that is less harsh than she feared. The heartwarming realisation finally comes, and Muriel no longer spends all day in her bedroom listening to Abba songs because her life has now become "as good as an Abba song".

Subtext: The seedy side of family life in Australia is explored in all its sordidness. The verbally abusive father leaves his wife for another woman and the wife subsequently kills herself. The daughter steals all his money for a holiday in Bali where she masquerades as the fiance of the imaginary Tim Sims. The son spends all of his time imagining he is a famous football player.

The daughter, Muriel, is the star of the show and the director focuses on her repeated humiliations. She is tormented by her corrupt politician father, shallow "friends" and her "mail order" husband.

Background: The film makes an interesting critique of the idealisms created around love, marriage and family relationships. Often billed as a comedy, satire would be a more accurate label. The brilliant direction comes courtesy of P.J. Hogan who helmed the famous *My Best Friend's Wedding* and worked as an assistant director for *How to Make an American Quilt*.

Muriel's Wedding is about exposing secrets, and the manner of its filming reflects this theme. The light is harsh, showing every flaw in the skin of its characters, and the scenery is gritty architecture juxtaposed with vibrant landscapes. The film's buoyancy comes from its music: after all, what scene could possibly be depressing while ABBA exalts Napoleon's surrender at Waterloo in the background?

It was nominated for awards at the BAFTA, Golden Globes, Writer's Guild USA and it won several awards at the AFI Awards.

Verdict: *Muriel's Wedding* is a cultural classic, well known in both Australia and in the UK. Beneath the funny one-liners and famous catch phrases – "you're terrible Muriel" – aspects of the film are quite disturbing. 3/5

Flynn (1996)

Directed by: Frank Howson

Written by: Alister Webb, Frank Howson

Produced by: Peter Boyle, Frank Howson, Jacques Kouri,

Malcolm Olivestone, Barbi Taylor, William J. Vass, James Michael Vernon

Edited by: Peter Carrodus, Peter McBain

Cinematography: John Wheeler

Cast: Guy Pearce (Errol Flynn), Claudia Karvan (Penelope Watts), Steven Berkoff (Klaus Reicher) 96 minutes

Story: This is a romanticised version of the early life of infamous actor Errol Flynn during the 1920s, portrayed here as a lover and a dreamer down on his luck until the classic film *In the Wake of the Bounty* showed his talent to Hollywood and made him a star.

Subtext: Read between the lines, and Flynn was a criminal, plagued by the IRS, with three rape charges to his name and a criminal history in the gold fields of PNG.

Background: A great cast, including Guy Pearce and Claudia Karvan, and an interesting premise, the historical biography of Flynn should have made for a blockbuster film. Unfortunately, the dawdling screenplay romanticises the events, and the direction of Frank Howson is less than cohesive.

Verdict: Worth a look if you're a fan of Flynn or Guy Pearce, the only great scene is of a very realistic boxing match carried off with gritty flair by Pearce. 2/5

Dating the Enemy (1996)

Directed and written by: Megan Simpson Huberman

Produced by: Phil Gerlach, Sue Miliken, Heather Ogilvie

Edited by: Marcus D'Arcy

Cinematography: Steve Arnold

Cast: Guy Pearce (Brett), Claudia Karvan (Tash) 95 minutes

Story: The battle of the sexes is a drama common to modern life. Is the grass greener on the other side? A woman might wish that men could experience menstruation, fastening a bra strap, premature ejaculation (from the receiving end), weight watching, or being treated like a secretary by male colleagues. Men might wish women could understand what it's like to be punched in the nose for defending someone's honour or cutting yourself shaving, ridiculed while playing basketball or criticised for talking about feelings.

Brett (Guy Pearce) and Tash (Claudia Karvan) experience just this when they swap bodies. It's an experience that allows both of them to fight the battle of the sexes from an extremely unique position. There are enemies in both camps and the war is waged not only in the office but also in their personal relationship. It's a comedy boosted by incredible acting, and a unique approach to a continuing struggle.

Subtext: The heartwarming revelations of the film are that opposites attract and that men and women should stop battling and work together. As Tash says, "It's like a three-legged race, if we go in opposite directions, we won't get anywhere."

Background: The film was a huge success in Australia probably due to the presence of Guy Pearce. Other big names in the credits were Sue Milliken, the producer who also made *Sirens* and David Hirschfelder, the composer who worked on *Strictly Ballroom*.

Verdict: If you've ever fantasised about living inside the body of someone of the opposite sex, you'll enjoy watching Guy Pearce play with his new breasts all day and Claudia Karvan as she runs around the house lifting furniture with one arm.

This film is yet another testament to the skill of Guy Pearce in a demanding role. 5/5

Occasional Coarse Language (1998)

Directed and written by: Brad Hayward

Produced by: Brendan Fletcher, Brad Hayward, Michael Lake, Joel Pearlman, Trish Piper

Edited by: Simon Martin

Cinematography: Rebecca Barry

Cast: Sara Browne (Min Rogers), Astrid Grant (Jazz), Nicholas Bishop (David), Michael Walker (Stanley), 81 minutes

Story: The success of Occasional Coarse Language was largely due to the dialogue written for Min Rogers (Sara Browne) who'll be "twenty-three the year after next", as she laments to her girlfriends over lunch. She is going through an early life crisis: her boyfriend is cheating on her, her flatmate has kicked her out, her boss has fired her, her dad has a hernia, and she isn't getting any sex. It's shocking: a young women who talks about sex and not only that, swears and smokes as well...

She never fails to tell us exactly how it is. She "wasn't dumped" she was "pissed on from a great height". She doesn't smoke because she has to but because "it looks so fucking cool"; she's "not one of these addictive types". And wait until you hear about the size of the suppository her mum has to insert into her father's arse.

Min's funniest disclosure comes after she unwittingly spends the night hiding under her nymphomaniac flatmate's bed while he sleeps with yet another "scantily clad malnourished starlet". She winges to her best friend Jazz, "I never realised that the sound of a woman having an orgasm could be so terrifying. It was like she was giving birth to a government bus or something. It's a miracle the bitch can even stand up... Then I walk out in the morning and she's sitting there looking like Cindy fucking Crawford after just enduring the sexual equivalent of the decathlon." Min confronts her flatmate with his problem and he defends himself saying that he is only sleeping around until he gets over his ex-girlfriend. Min's response: "By the time you get over Jessica you'll have impregnated half the Pacific Rim."

Subtext: "Australian morals protection authority warning: for safety and comfort viewers are reminded that the following program may contain sequences involving medium level conjugal sex of a gratuitous nature." Right from the beginning this film takes the piss out of censorship laws. It also flaunts social etiquette as often as possible. The director, Brett Hayward, commented that people found it affronting, especially male reviewers. He mentioned however that female viewers loved it with particular emphasis on older women (40–60) who found the film hilarious.

Background: As Hayward's first film, it was extremely low budget, made with second-hand equipment, borrowed money and inexperienced actors. A recipe for disaster, in the end grossed it extremely well at the cinema, confounding all expectations.

Despite its low budget, the film is creative in its editing using snapshot sequences supplemented with an amazing soundtrack of young Australian rock artists, which gave the movie most of its notoriety.

Verdict: The film has a certain realism sometimes lacking in popular Hollywood films. Average girls falling in love with average guys actually look average and don't have bleached teeth or plastic faces; hungover actresses will wake up after a big night partying with make-up smeared over their faces in a reassuring rainbow of ugliness.

One drawback, however, is that the director could only afford to shoot one take, so some of the supporting actors' scenes leave a little to be desired. This is particularly noticeable during the overly-emotional ending, otherwise saved by Min's final comments to her mother, "Did you end up finding the thermometer you thought you'd left up his (arse)?" 4/5

Siam Sunset (1999)

Directed by: Jon Polson

Written by: Max Dann, Andrew Knight

Produced by: Peter Beilby, Al Clark, Andrew Knight, Max Dann

Edited by: Nicholas Beauman

Cinematography: Brian Breheny

Cast: Linus Roache (Perry), Danielle Cormack (Grace), Ian Bliss (Martin), Roy Billing (Bill Leach), Alan Brough (Stuart Quist), Rebecca Hobbs (Jane), Terry Kenwrick (Arthur Droon), Deidre Rubenstein (Celia Droon), Peter Hosking (Roy Wentworth), Victoria Eagger (Rowena Wentworth), Robert Menzies (Eric), Eliza Lovell (Michelle), Heidi Glover (Stephanie Droon), Lachlan Standing (Ben Wentworth), Esme Melville (Dot) 91 minutes

Story: Perry is relaxing on his front lawn when a refrigerator drops from the sky and kills his wife. Some would say this is a funny way to open a movie and others would say it's twisted. *Siam Sunset* is a bit of both. Perry falls victim to a supernatural phenomenon whereby dangerous natural and unnatural disasters are attracted to his person. When he tries to escape to the Australian outback things get a whole lot worse (imagine floods, snakes, fires and two crazy tour operators who are racing each other to the top of Australia). And then the girl-friend of a homicidal drug dealer decides to get the hots for Perry and it's a disaster prone match made in heaven.

Subtext: This film really pokes fun at Australia, "the idealised holiday setting": a tour bus gets stuck in the desert due to floods and the entire group is forced to live on beetroot for weeks on end. It also pokes fun at the stereotypical 'whingeing Pom' with the caricatured wimpy British man, Perry. On a more serious note the two lovebirds find Siam Sunset, "the colour of peace", in their relationship with each other while the world around them continues in dangerous chaos.

Background: A hilarious film, its two writers are well known for their television comedy work in productions such as *Full Frontal, Fast Forward, Sea Change, Shaun Micallef* and *Jimeoin*. Director John Polson, also a well-known actor and musician, whose other famous films include *The Sum of Us, Mission Impossible* and *Sirens*, won an award at the Cannes Film Festival for *Siam Sunset*. There are some great performances, especially by Roy Billing and Ian Bliss, who went on to star in *The Matrix* films.

Verdict: A superbly timed comedy backed up by a tight script and a star cast. 4/5

1997–2006
Contemporary Films

The long arduous road of Australian cinema is reaping its rewards in the country's contemporary films. Everything that has been put in over the last century is coming out with prolific clarity.

Gillian Armstrong continues to make award-winning films with strong female characters. She started in the 1970s with *My Brilliant Career*, more recently gave us *Oscar and Lucinda*, and one of her legacies is new director Cate Shortland and her film *Somersault* (2004).

In 1966 *They're a Weird Mob* paved the way for contemporary films about immigration, and migrant decedents, especially of ethnic backgrounds. Films such as *Soft Fruit*, *Lantana* and *Looking for Alibrandi* have since shown us ethnic characters with stories of mental anguish. The latest film about racial difference, *Japanese Story*, continues the legacy of cinematographer Ian Baker whose beginnings were in *The Chant of Jimmie Blacksmith*.

Australians are descended from convicts and bushrangers and proud of it. There has always been a strong contingent of crime films and the recent industry is no different: Heath Ledger in *Ned Kelly* (2003) and *Two Hands* (1999); Eric Banner in *Chopper* (2000); *Let's Get Skase* (2001); *Dirty Deeds* (2002), *The Nugget* (2002) and recent success *Gettin' Square*.

The legacy of *Mad Max* and its cinematographer, David Eggby, is prominent in the latest desert sci-fi flick, *Pitch Black*.

The horror of the early 1970s is revisited in *Wolf Creek* and *Undead* (2001).

Comedy has always been a mainstay of Australian art. Whether it's a war film such as *Breaker Morant* or a settler film such as *Dad and Dave*, a sense of humour has kept Aussie characters strong and human. The recent comedy *The Castle* (1997) is already an Australian classic as is the tragi-comedy set in World War Two, *Changi* (2001).

Let us not forget the sexual revolution, which Nicole Kidman and Baz Luhrmann drew on in their risqué art house film about a cabaret dancer, *Moulin Rouge*.

After the bold beginnings of *Jedda* (1955), indigenous Australians are now raising their voice even louder with *Rabbit-Proof Fence*.

The Australian film industry has become what it always deserved to be. It includes and spans a cross-section of historical themes and Aussie archetypes. And the talented artists that work within it sometimes even get paid.

The Castle (1997)

Directed by: Rob Sitch

Written by: Santo Cilauro, Tom Gleisner, Jane Kennedy, Rob Sitch

Produced by: Michael Hirsh, Debra Choate

Edited by: Wayne Hyett

Cinematography: Miriana Marusic

Cast: Michael Caton (Darryl Kerrigan), Anne Tenney (Sal Kerrigan), Stephen Curry (Dale Kerrigan), Anthony Simcoe (Steve Kerrigan), Sophie Lee (Tracey Kerrigan), Wayne Hope

(Wayne Kerrigan), Tiriel Mora (Dennis Denuto), Eric Bana (Con Petropoulous), Charles Bud Tingwell (Laurence Hammill), Robyn Nevin (Federal Court Judge), Costas Kilias (Farouk), Bryon Dawe (Ron Graham), Monty Maizels (Jack), Lynda Gibson (Evonne), John Benton (Mr Lyle) 82 minutes

Story: Darryl Kerrigan's "house is his home and a man's home is his castle"; but the government is trying to take it away from him. This is a hilarious battle between the big guys and the Little Aussie Battlers who just want the right to live in their own home. As Darryl says, "This government has got to learn to stop taking other people's land." "It's Mabo, it's the constitution, it's the vibe…" his 'lawyer' tells the high court.

Subtext: Apart from references to Aboriginal land rights and anti-authoritarian sentiments in Australia, this film also looks closely at the lives of ordinary Australians and often-comedic simple pleasures, for example, a holiday house on a dam out in Woop Woop, where a family can enjoy the 'serenity' of a two-stroke engine.

Background: Produced on an extremely low budget, props and sets were borrowed and filming lasted eleven days, at which point the money ran out. Despite these obvious hurdles the film was a huge success in Australia, owing much to the humorous screenplay and comedy timing of the actors and director.

Verdict: The funniest film to come out of Australia yet. 5/5

Oscar and Lucinda (1998)

Directed by: Gillian Armstrong

Written by: Peter Carey (novel), Laura Jones (screenplay)

Produced by: Robin Dalton, Mark Turnbull, Timothy White

Edited by: Nicholas Beauman

Cinematography: Geoffrey Simpson

Cast: Ralph Fiennes (Oscar Hopkins), Cate Blanchett (Lucinda Leplastrier), Ciaran Hinds (Rev Dennis Hasset), Tom Wilkinson (Hugh Stratton), Richard Roxburgh (Mr Jeffries), Clive Russell (Theophilus), Billy Brown (Percy Smith), Josephine Byrnes (Mirium Chadwick), Barnaby Kay (Wardley-Fish), Barry Otto (Jimmy D'Abbs), Linda Bassett (Bett Stratton), Geoffrey Rush (Narrator), Polly Cheshire (Young Lucinda), Gillian Jones (Elizabeth Leplastrier), Robert Menzies (Abel Leplastrier) 126 minutes.

Story: Cate Blanchett plays Lucinda, a wealthy heiress who has a gambling addiction and a penchant for priests. Ralph Fiennes is Oscar, a nineteenth Century Anglican priest who believes that gambling is divine because his basic belief in religion is based on a gamble he made as a child. The two meet and are shunned for their risqué behavior. Eventually they make a large wager to build a glass church and transport it to a faraway outback town. Oscar wins the bet and arrives at the town only to die tragically when the church sinks into the river while he is trapped inside. His mentor, an older Anglican priest, hangs himself because of a gambling addiction.

Subtext: The glass church represents the fragile and transparent nature of religion which has enclosed and finally killed its most devoted followers. Lucinda represents the free spirited new Australian who broke the rules of nineteenth century England to raise the illegitimate son of Oscar into a proud, modern Australian. Pascal's Wager is also visited.

SASKIA VANDERBENT

Background: An Academy Award® nominee, the movie is based on the Booker Prize-winning novel of the same name, written by multiple award-winning author, Peter Carey whose most recent award was the 2001 Booker for *The History of the Kelly Gang*. Carey is famous for his controversial attitudes towards the mother country (England) and is a strong republican who refused to accept an invitation from the Queen on one occasion and postponed a meeting with her on a second occasion, forcing her to cancel in order to save face. Director Gillian Armstrong also has a history of controversy, stemming from her debut, *My Brilliant Career*, based on the feminist novel by Miles Franklin. Interestingly, Peter Carey has won the Miles Franklin Award for literature three times.

Cate Blanchett, another big name in Australia, is well known for her more commercial ventures such as *The Lord of the Rings*. English actor Ralph Fiennes made a name for himself in the film *The English Patient*.

Verdict: If you don't usually have the stomach for historical, romantic dramas you may still enjoy this film. With a brilliant screenplay, it is delivered by wonderful actors under the flawless and artistic direction of Gillian Armstrong, who always captures the essence of the Australian experience through the expression of her own passion. 4/5

Soft Fruit (1999)

Directed by: Christina Andreef

Written by: Christina Andreef

Produced by: Helen Bowden, Jane Campion

Edited by: Jane Moran

Cinematography: Laszlo Baranyai

Cast: Jeanie Drynan (Patsy), Linal Haft (Vic), Russell Dykastra (Bo), Genevieve Lemon (Josie), Sacha Horler (Nadia), Alicia Talbot (Vera), Dion Bilios (Bud), Gezelle Byrnes (Elly), Jordon Franklin (Thomas), Cheyenne Dobbs (Gertie), Marin Mimica (Swifty), Glenn Butcher (Tony), Terry Weaver (Podge), Trevor Mills (Smudge) 100 minutes

Story: A mother who has provided the only peace and happiness for her children in the face of an abusive father is dying. When her children come home to be with her in her last days, the important role that she has played in their lives becomes apparent. Slowly she takes centre-stage and her husband the backseat. Eventually she leaves her husband, if only for one night of peace, before she dies.

Central to the family's life is the son, Bo, who seemed to take the worst of the beatings from his father while growing up and who is banished to the shed when he returns on parole for his mother's final days.

Bo, when abused by his father, escapes to his motorcycle outlaw friends where he abuses himself with drugs and criminal activity. The cycle of abuse becomes worse as everyone tries to escape from the father while he stockpiles cans of food, locking himself in his house and shooting birds from the window, a crazy man who can't let go of his fear of war.

Although the plot sounds dark, the result is a lighthearted comedy. There are some surreal moments when Bo and his mother tour the town together, high on morphine. The father, while abusive, is portrayed in a farcical manner. The daughters are also hilarious, constantly dieting and worrying about their ticking biological clocks.

Subtext: The son, Bo (Russell Dykstra), has an interesting theory about why he puts up with his abusive father. When his outlaw mates ask him to come hang out with them he says, "I'm keeping my nose clean for me old ma, she's crook..." "Where's that cunt of an old man of yours?" they ask him.

"I ain't got nothing against me old man," he says, "See that lawn? It's full of bindis. Bindis that stop the cat dead in the middle of it. I'm in training so I can walk straight through it. People with soft feet can't do that, do you know why? They wear socks and shoes all the time. It's a matter of putting up with a little bit of pain. I want to get so I can walk along the road when it's baking hot, on the hot tar, not the nice smooth tar but the rocky, hot, boiling tar. Cunts will say 'Why don't you walk beside it, on the grass?' and I'll say, 'Cause sooner or later cunt, I'm gunna have to cross the road again and my feet are gunna complain.'"

Background: This film won awards at the Sydney film festival, San Sebastian, Turin, and the AFI Awards. Christina Andreef worked on two big films, *The Piano* and *Crush* prior to directing *Soft Fruit*, and the atmosphere of the film owes much to the experienced editor, Jane Moran, and her artistic sequencing; she has worked as an assistant and first assistant editor on such films as *Dark City*, *Bootmen*, *Strictly Ballroom*, *Muriel's Wedding* and *Moulin Rouge*.

Verdict: This is one of the only films to adequately capture the atmosphere of the suburban, Sydney garden setting through its colour, camera movement and shot design. Very funny moments of surrealism and a meaningful screenplay add up to a great piece of art. 4/5

Two Hands (1999)

Directed by: Gregor Jordan

Written by: Gregor Jordan

Produced by: Marian Macgowan, Bryce Menzies, Mark Turnbull, Timothy White

Edited by: Lee Smith

Cinematography: Malcolm McCulloch

Cast: Heath Ledger (Jimmy), Bryan Brown (Pando), Rose Byrne (Alex), Susie Porter (Deidre), Steven Vidler (Michael), David Field (Acko), Tom Long (Wally), Tony Forrow (Eddie), Mariel McClorey (Helen), Evan Sheaves (Pete), Steve Le Marquand (Wozza), Kiri Paramore (Les), Kieran Darcey-Smith (Craig), Mathew Wilkinson (Rocket), Mary Acres (Mrs Jones) 103 minutes

Story: Heath Ledger is Jimmy, a young guy who gets involved with the local crime gang in Kings Cross, Sydney. When the money he is supposed to be transporting gets stolen, his life is worth about as much as his brother's, who was killed working for the same criminal gang. A friend looking to steal his job and his girlfriend help the crooks to chase Jimmy while a young homeless kid, whose friend was killed by the same crooks, looks for revenge.

Subtext: The film explores the criminal underground of Sydney and its links to homeless and unemployed kids on the streets.

Background: A polished production with fantastic direction that saw Heath Ledger treading in the acting career footsteps of Mel Gibson. He has since been in American films such as *Ten Things I Hate About You*, *Monster's Ball* and *The Patriot*. The director's only other mildly successful film has been *Ned Kelly*, which also starred Ledger.

Two Hands is one of the most contemporary Aussie films to date, from the soundtrack, featuring rock legends Powder

Finger, to the expertise of editor Lee Smith (*The Truman Show, Turtle Beach, Buffalo Soldiers*), who gave the film its professional polish. It was made with an extremely experienced crew, with casting by Christine King (*Rabbit-Proof Fence, The Quiet American*), production design by Steven Jones-Evans, and art direction by Richard Hobbs.

Verdict: The Tarantino style plot twists and character development techniques are given a unique Aussie spin here. The perennial theme of criminals as heroes has become outdated, as Australia has increasingly taken on a more American view point that law breakers are the bad guys, although this doesn't go as far as being a cops and robbers flick. 5/5

Chopper (2000)

Directed by: Andrew Dominik

Written by: Mark Brandon Read (books), Andrew Dominik

Produced by: Michael Bennett, Al Clark, Martin Fabinyi, Michael Gudinski, Yvonne Collins

Edited by: Ken Sallows

Cinematography: Geoffrey Hall, Kevin Hayward

Cast: Eric Bana (Mark Brandon 'Chopper' Read), Simon Lyndon (Jimmy Loughnan), David Field (Keithy George), Daniel Wyllie (Bluey), Bill Young (Det. Downie), Vince Colosimo (Neville Bartos), Kenny Graham (Keith Read), Kate Behan (Tanya), Serge Liistro (Sammy the Turk), Pam Western (Tanya's Mother), Garry Waddell (Kevin Darcey), Brian Mannix (Ian James), Skye Wansey (Mandy), Annalise Emtsis (Shazzy) 94 minutes

Story: Chopper Read, the notorious criminal from Melbourne, became a legend after his book *From the Inside* was released. It was a bestseller, which amused Chopper who had never finished school. The film follows Chopper's earlier criminal life and also his life within the prison, where he wrote the book. Many of his stories contradict each other and he is well known for telling different versions of the same crime in order to confuse the police about which version might be the truth. There are some great scenes: Chopper (played by Bana) slicing his ears to get into the prison hospital, and an entertaining show down between Chopper and Neville Bartos (Vince Colosimo) towards the end.

Subtext: Australian audiences love a Ned Kelly symbol. Chopper definitely has charisma and a sense of humour which made him a legendary anti-authority figure.

Background: The film was also popular internationally. It helped Eric Bana to land subsequent roles in Hollywood in films such as *Hulk* and *Troy*, although he was already quite famous in Australia for his work in *Full Frontal* and *The Castle*. Vince Colosimo's first big film was the fantastic comedy *Wog Boy* but *Chopper* made way for his roles in classic films such as *Lantana*, *Walking on Water* and *The Hard Word*.

Verdict: Acted, directed and shot with perfect realism and a touch of dark humour. 4.5/5

Pitch Black (2000)

Directed by: David Twohy

Written by: Jim Wheat, Ken Wheat, David Twohy

Produced by: Tony Winley, Scott Kroopf, Ted Field, Tom Engelman

Edited by: Rick Shaine

Cinematography: David Eggby

Cast: Vin Diesel (Richard B. Riddick), Radha Mitchell (Carolyn Fry), Cole Hauser (William J. Johns), Keith David (Abu Imam al-Walid), Lewis Fitzgerald (Paris P. Ogilvie), Claudia Black (Sharon Montgomery), Rhiana Griffith (Jack, Jackie), John Moore (John), Simon Burke (Greg Owens) 110 minutes

Story: A spaceship crashes on an unknown planet. Among the principle survivors are the pilot, Carolyn (Radha Mitchell), and bounty hunter Johns (Cole Hauser). His bounty is the freaky-eyed criminal, Riddick (Vin Diesel). Riddick has animal-like reflector screens at the back of his eyes that enable him to see in the dark, which is just as well as because the inhabitants of the planet are bloodthirsty aliens which only come out at night and the planet is about to enter an eternal eclipse.

Another of the survivors is a young boy, Jack (Rhiana Griffith), who turns out, in true sci-fi fashion, to be a girl in baggy clothes. The girl is menstruating and the alien beasts smell her blood.

The ending is the controversial aspect of the story. Both principal characters, the pilot and Riddick the criminal, have previously sacrificed human life to save their own skins and each must learn compassion and the value of other human life. Carolyn learns it in time to sacrifice herself for the criminal Riddick and he learns it just in time to watch her die.

Subtext: The strong female lead is killed off and Vin Diesel is left alive to make a sequel. Something good comes of her life sacrifice, however: he becomes a reformed man and decides to be less selfish.

Background: American David Twohy directed and wrote this film and deserves full credit for his contribution to the science fiction genre. Experienced New Zealand musician, Graham Revelle, who has worked on more than 85 productions including *Dead Calm, Bangkok Hilton, The Crow, The Saint, Tank Girl, Dune, Lara Croft* and *Daredevil*, provided the score.

Verdict: Made through a collaboration of Australian and American filmmakers, this a good example of the flamboyant artistic creativity and free ideas of America mixed with the realism and down to earth humanity of Australian ideals. It also uses the bare Australian desert as a backdrop, the same location as its sci-fi predecessor *Mad Max*, and both films shared cinematographer David Eggby. He was aided by the production design of Grace Walker, known mostly for the films *Dead Calm, Mad Max Beyond Thunderdome, The Sum of Us* and *Crocodile Dundee*. Well-known art director, Ian Gracie, and the long list of animators and designers also deserve mention. The technology used was developed by the filmmakers of *Babe* and developed further by the Australian filmmakers in *The Matrix* films. It loses a point, however, for the opening scene, a sci-fi cliché that should have been forever relegated to the history books by Mel Brook's *Space Balls*. 4/5

Looking for Alibrandi (2001)

Directed by: Kate Woods

Written by: Malina Marchetta (also novel)

Produced by: Robyn Kershaw, Tristram Miall

Edited by: Martin Connor

Cinematography: Toby Oliver

Cast: Pia Miranda (Josi Alibrandi), Greta Scacchi (Christina Alibrandi), Anthony LaPaglia (Michael Andretti), Elena Cotta (Katie Alibrandi), Kick Gurry (Jacob Coote), Matthew Newton (John Barton) 103 minutes

Story: Final year of high school is hard at the best of times but Josie (Pia Miranda) has it worse than most. She has an Italian grandmother to contend with and a long lost father who suddenly shows up and if that isn't enough her best friend commits suicide.

Subtext: This film confronts teenage depression, suicide, family conflict and racism towards Italian immigrants.

Background: *Looking for Alibrandi* is a teen flick based on the popular novel often used as part of the Australian high school English curriculum.

Verdict: A necessary film for all Australian teenagers, this film confronts real problems that are often swept under the rug. 4/5

Changi (2001)

Directed by: Kate Woods

Written by: John Doyle

Produced by: Bill Hughs, Tim Pye

Edited by: Christopher Spurr

Cinematography: Joseph Pickering

Cast: Stephen Curry (Eddie), Leon Ford (Bill Dwyer), Anthony Hayes (Gordon Yates), Matthew Newton (David Collins), Mark Priestley (John 'Curley' Foster), Matthew Whittet (Tom), Geoff Morrell (Rowdy Lawson) 360 minutes (mini-series)

Story: Towards the end of World War Two thousands of allied troops were killed by their Japanese captors in Asian POW camps, through starvation, beatings, overwork (particularly on the Burma-Thailand railway) torture and forced marches.

Changi, Singapore, was one of the most notorious POW camps in Asia. This film is fictionally based on the Changi camp and follows the imprisonment of six of the Australian troops and their fight for survival. It documents the torture that killed them as well as the mateship, sabotage and escape attempts that helped them to survive.

Subtext: Australian troops typically out-survived and out-endured prisoners of other nationalities in POW camps. One such case was the Sandakan camp where six out of the 2700 allied prisoners survived, all of them Australian escapees. This film was intended to capture the Australian spirit, sense of humour and teamwork that enabled them to out-suffer the other prisoners.

Background: The director, Kate Woods, was also responsible for the classic, *Looking for Alibrandi*. She has a pattern of representing Australians as surviving horrifying or dark experiences through humour.

John Doyle, usually a television comedy writer, and Stephen Curry, a comedy actor, famous for films such as *The Castle* and *Nugget*, both lent their comedy to this piece, which could otherwise have been unremittingly dark.

Verdict: A moving film about Australian suffering and the strength of the human spirit. 5/5

Lantana (2001)

Directed by: Ray Lawrence

Written by: Andrew Bovell (also play)

Produced by: Jan Chapman, Catherine Jarman, Rainer Mockert, Mikael Borglund

Edited by: Karl Sodersten

Cinematography: Mandy Walker

Cast: Anthony La Paglia (Detective Leon Zat), Rachael Blake (Jane O'May), Kerry Armstrong (Sonja Zat), Melissa Martinez (Lisa), Owen McKenna (Old man in pyjamas), (Nicholas Cooper (Sam Zat), Marc Dwyer (Dylan Zat), Puven Pather (Drug dealer), Geoffrey Rush (John Knox), Peter Phelps (Patrick Phelan), Ashley Fitzgerald (Elanor), Vince Colosimo (Nik Daniels), Daniella Farinacci (Paula Daniels), Keira Wingate (Hannah Daniels), Russel Dykstra (Michael), Glenn Robbins (Pete O'May) 121 minutes

Story: The indiscretions and dishonesty involved in the relationships of several middle-aged couples are complicated when John Knox's wife disappears. The local 'ethnic', Nik Daniels (Vince Colosimo), is blamed as he is observed throwing a woman's shoe into some lantana scrub.

A jealous neighbour who likes to fantasise about Nik, asks his wife Paula, "How do you know he didn't do it?" Paula looks at her with absolute disgust and responds: "Because he told me."

In contrast, when detective Leon Zat cheats on his wife, he cannot understand that her trust has been shattered, not by the sexual act, but by the fact that he lied to her about it.

Subtext: It is ironic that the only couple that isn't trusted in the community is the 'foreign couple', Nik and his wife Paula, and they are the only people that are true and loyal to each other despite the degree to which their loyalty is tested. Like the flowering lantana bush, considered to be a noxious weed in New South Wales, they were not originally native to Australia yet they are here and they are beautiful.

Background: *Lantana* won multiple awards and is known for its sizeable cast of well-known and loved Aussie actors.

Verdict: Shot through with atmosphere, you can practically smell the lantana and feel the emotion of the characters. One of the great contemporary films. 5/5

Moulin Rouge (2001)

Directed by: Baz Luhrmann

Written by: Baz Luhrmann, Craig Pearce

Produced by: Baz Luhrmannn, Catherine Martin, Catherine Knapman, Martin Brown, Fred Baron, Steve Andrews

Edited by: Jil Bilcock

Cinematography: Donald McAlpine

Cast: Nicole Kidman (Satine), Ewan McGregor (Christian), John Leguizamo (Toulous-Lautrec), Jim Broadbent (Harold Zidler), Richard Roxburg (The Duke), Garry McDonald

(The Doctor), Kylie Minogue (The Green Fairy) 127 minutes

Story: A poet and a courtesan are forced to choose between their love for each other and their love for their different art forms. While the poet (Ewan MacGregor) has no trouble choosing, the dancer (Nicole Kidman) struggles with her choice and finally, dying of syphilis, cuts that struggle short.

Subtext: The choice between art and life is explored, as well as the artist's choice to sell their soul and body for success and recognition.

Background: *Moulin Rouge* had an extravagant budget, and Baz Luhrmann takes the credit for the success of the production. Considering this was a period piece, his definitive style of bright colours, excessive costumes, fast paced sequencing, bold music and over the top acting was brave, imbuing the film with an atmosphere akin to sci-fi and confounding audience expectation. It is an improvement on his classic film *Strictly Ballroom*, which caused waves in 1992.

Verdict: An extravagant production filled with bright colours, inspiring soundtracks and creativity. 5/5

Let's Get Skase (2001)

Directed by: Matthew George

Written by: Matthew George, Lachy Hulme

Produced by: Judy Mamgren, Joel Pearlman, Colin South, John Tatoulis

Edited by: Michael Collins

Cinematography: Justin Brickle

Cast: Lachy Hulme (Peter Dellasandro), Alex Dimitriades (Danny D'Amato Jr.), Craig McLachlan (Eric Carney), Adam Haddrick (Rupert Wingate), Torquil Neilson (Sean Knight), Nick Sheppard (Dave Phibbs), William Ten Eyck (Dick Rydell), Vince D'Amico (Daniel D'Amato Sr.), Bill Kerr (Mitchell Vendieks), George Shevtsov (Beneheim Bencini), Gordon Honeycombe (Murray Bishop), Helen Buday (Judith Turner), Vivienne Garrett (Ruth D'Amato), Nick Atkinson (Anthony D'Amato), Wayne Hassell (Christopher Skase) 96 minutes

Story: Christopher Skase was an Australian criminal who stole millions of dollars in corporate crime and then fled to Majorca, from whence he never returned despite much time and money spent by the Australian government to extradite him. This is a comedy about a homemade SWAT team that sets out to kidnap Christopher Skase and bring him back to Australia. They seek justice, they seek money and they seek retribution.

Subtext: Skase was the antithesis of the Ned Kelly criminal. Instead of being anti-authority, he held a lot of authority himself. He was a big-business, rich, corporate type who often bribed the media and fled the country while still owing Australia $40 million.

Background: The actors and director are not well known apart from Craig McLachlan who is perhaps best remembered for having dated Kylie Minogue in his youth.

Verdict: Despite a funny screenplay, delivered well, it was released the same year as Skase's death and left a slightly awkward taste in the mouths of the audience. 3.5/5

Undead (2001)

Directed by: The Spierig Brothers

Written by: The Spierig Brothers

Produced by: Michael Spierig, Peter Spierig

Edited by: Michael Spierig, Peter Spierig

Cinematography: Andrew Strahorn

Cast: Felicity Mason (Rene), Mungo McKay (Marion), Rob Jenkins (Wayne), Lisa Cunningham (Sallyanne), Dirk Hunter (Harrison), Emma Randall (Molly), Steve Grieg (Agent) 104 minutes

Story: Filmed on the Gold Coast but set in a fictional fishing village, *Undead* draws from classic gore-filled speculative fiction films such as *Braindead* and *Dawn of the Dead*. The screenplay starts off on a contrived and amateurish note but kicks in mid-way with some comic dialogue and supernatural twists. The main characters are very original. Meet Marion, the crazy fisherman gunslinger who is tormented by an alien abduction that occurred in his past, and Rene, the beauty queen who is not just a pretty face but the chosen one, picked to protect the town from the zombies.

Subtext: As usual in Aussie film, the cops are the bad guys in Aussie films. The two in *Undead* are particularly anally retentive and obnoxious although they provide some hilarious dialogue. When the Constable first spots the zombies descending on their hideout he curses: "It's all those fucking crack marijuana fucking hippie fucking surfie fucking dole-bludging pricks – fuck!"; a perfect comedic summary of the police-force's attitude towards the general populace.

Marion is the town crazy man who turns out to be a gun-slinging hero, and Rene is the town pauper who turns out to be a beauty queen/zombie slayer, expounding the theme of earlier Australian horror films that those who are deemed "crazy" or "outsiders" are often the most valuable, the most aware of what is going on.

Usually in a zombie film the zombies represent the horror of flock mentality within society. Not so here: a zombie is the only person in the town to escape, returned to doom the town with re-infection after everyone else had been cured. The individual then is the town's downfall.

A tongue in cheek conversion of the ordinarily nauseating stereotypical bimbo beauty queen that saturates the Gold Coast culture, particularly enjoyable is the final scene where Rene sits on her porch guarding the townspeople while they wait for the symbolic cleansing rains that will cure them from the zombie virus. It is a familiar feeling for Queenslanders who spend most of their years in drought, hoping for rains that never come.

Background: Considering its low budget, the results are amazing. The directors undertook all of the computer animation and graphics work: their computers often didn't have the processing power to render a single shot and would crash, on average, fifteen times per day. The visual effects had to be creative because no money was available after the first day of shooting. Shooting ended when the film ran out, and most of the cast and crew were unpaid. Yet the enthusiasm carried through so that the end product looks like a high budget film.

Verdict: Concerns that this may be a poor version of the New Zealand classic *Braindead* were soon quashed. The computer graphics are mind-blowing, the comedy is well timed and the characters original. The gun slinging fisherman is a breath of fresh air; particularly enjoyable is watching him back flip, and dig his spurs into the plaster so that he can hang upside down from the door frame in order to shoot zombies from this clearly improved vantage point. 4/5

Rabbit-Proof Fence (2002)

Directed by: Phillip Noyce

Written by: Doris Pilkington (novel), Christine Olsen

Produced by: Laura Burrows, David Elfick, Kathleen McLaughlin, Philip Noyce, Christine Olsen, Emile Sherman, Jonathan Shteinman, Jeremy Thomas, John Winter, Oliver Huzley

Edited by: Veronika Jenet, John Scott

Cinematography: Christopher Doyle

Cast: Everlyn Sampi (Molly Craig), Tianna Sansbury (Daisy Kadibill), Laura Monagham (Gracie Fields), David Gulpilil (Moodoo Tracker), Ningali Lawford (Maud), Myarn Lawford (Molly's Grandmother), Deborah Mailman (Mavis), Jason Clarke (Constable Riggs), Kenneth Branagh (A.O.Neville), Natasha Wanganeen (Nina), Garry McDonald (Neal), Roy Billing (Police Inspector), Lorna Leslie (Miss Thomas), Celine O'Leary (Miss Jessop), Kate Roberts (Matron) 94 minutes

Story: Molly and her sister Gracie escape from one of the Christian mission homes of the 1930s. They set off on a 1500-mile trek across the outback to find their mother from whom they have been stolen.

Subtext: This story comes from the book by Doris Pilkington and follows the childhood of her mother, Molly Craig (played by Everlyn Sampi). Molly is one of the stolen generation of the 1930s, taken from her aboriginal mother along with her baby sister by the Reverend Neville for a life in the Christian Missions. Here they were taught to behave like white people, often sent to work for white families where they were sometimes raped and abused.

Background: Consummate casting by Christine King and art direction by Laurie Faen (*Sirens, Young Einstein*), together with such a well-written story, and experienced director Philip Noyce (see *Dead Calm*), ensured a high professional and artistic standard.

The film won a total of 19 major film awards and was nominated for another 18 besides. These included wins at the Sao Paulo International Film Festival, San Francisco Film Critics Circle and the London Film Critics Circle.

Verdict: Finally the story of the stolen generation has been told by an aboriginal voice and given a screen presence. This film is testament to the distance Australians have come since *The Chant of Jimmie Blacksmith* and the distance they still must travel. 5/5

Dirty Deeds (2002)

Directed by: David Caesar

Written by: David Caesar

Produced by: Deborah Balderstone, Bryan Brown, Xavier Marchand, Kris Noble, Jeanie Hughs, Hugh Marks, Richard Schor, Helen Watts

Edited by: Mark Perry

Cinematography: Geoffrey Hall

Cast: Bryan Brown (Barry Ryan), Toni Collette (Sharon), John Goodman (Tony), Sam Neil (Ray), Sam Worthington (Darcy), Kestie Morassi (Margaret), William McInnes (Hollywood), Andrew S. Gilbert (Norm), Gary Waddell (Freddy), Felix Williamson (Sal), Derek Amer (Manager), Laeini Baille (Coin Lady), Rudi Baker (Bell Boy), Bille Brown (Senator) 110 minutes

Story: Some members of the Chicago mafia decide to cash in on Aussie crime. However they didn't count on having to contend with Bryan Brown and his group of Aussie crooks. Set in the outback in the 1960s during the Vietnam War, the film deals with American multi-nationalism. It is the beginning of globalisation. A young Australian soldier, Darcy (Sam Worthington), gets his first taste of American pizza in Vietnam. His dream is to one day open a pizza shop in Australia. His Uncle, a local crime boss (Bryan Brown) doesn't agree. He doesn't think that people would buy the same type of food every time they went to a restaurant. He would prefer his nephew to follow in his own footsteps as a high-rolling criminal.

Subtext: This film is about American globalisation of crime syndicates, business and the American war machine that exports American business to the world.

Background: Shauna Wolifson deserves credit as the casting director and has had much success prior to and since *Dirty Deeds*, notably on *The Matrix* series, *Walking on Water, Mullet, Me Myself & I, Dark City* and *Idiot Box.* This is an all-star cast including American and Australian actors. Look out for John

Goodman, Toni Colette, Bryan Brown and Sam Neill among others.

Verdict: An interesting gangster-style film with a few funny plot twists. 3/5

The Nugget (2002)

Directed by: Bill Bennett

Written by: Bill Bennett

Produced by: Richard Sheffield, Bill Bennett, Jennifer Cluff, Ann Folland, Silvana Milat, Richard Sheffield

Edited by: Henry Dangar

Cinematography: Danny Ruhlmann

Cast: Eric Bana (Lotto), Stephen Curry (Wookie), Dave O'Neil (Sue), Belinda Emmett (Cheryl), Peter Moon (Ratner), Vince Colosimo (Dimitri), Max Cullen (Wally), Karen Pang (Moon Choo), Sallyanne Ryan (Darlene), Jurgen (Alan Brough), Jeff Trumen (George), Chris Haywood (George), Jean Kittson (Joyce), Glenda Linscott (Bunny), Jane Hall (Lucy) 97 minutes

Story: A group of road workers discover a gold nugget worth millions. They quit their jobs and start planning retirement, spending the money before they have even cashed in the gold. Meanwhile their wives find out and all hell breaks loose as they fight for who owns the nugget.

Subtext: Don't count your chickens before they've hatched. Don't let money affect your integrity. If you get married, your wife will turn your mates against you and you won't be able to have fun anymore... and other similar stereotypes and clichés.

Background: Bill Bennett is not a well-known director or writer and the only film of his worth mentioning is *Spider and Rose*. It's unfortunate that *Nugget* has such a bad screenplay, which did much more harm than good to most of the up and coming actors involved.

Verdict: With a star comedy cast including guys like Vince Colosimo (*Lantana, Chopper, The Wog Boy*), Eric Bana (*Troy, Hulk, Chopper, The Castle*), Stephen Curry (*Changi, The Wog Boy, The Castle*) audiences expected much more. As a new age fable it did okay but as a comedy it flopped big time. It just wasn't funny. 2/5

Ned Kelly (2003)

Directed by: Gregor Jordon

Written by: Robert Drewe (novel), John M. McDonagh

Produced by: Tim Bevan, Catherin Bishop, Liza Chasin, Robert Drewe, Eric Fellner, Debra Hayward, Lynda House, Timothy White, Nelson Woss

Edited by: Jon Gregory

Cinematography: Oliver Stapleton

Cast: Heath Ledger (Ned Kelly), Orlando Bloom (Joe Byrne), Geoffrey Rush (Francis Hare), Naomi Watts (Julia Cook), Joel Edgerton (Aaron Sherritt), Laurence Kinlan (Dan Kelly), Phil Barantini (Steve Hart), Kerry Condon (Kate

Kelly), Kris McQuade (Ellen Kelly), Emily Browning (Grace Kelly), Kiri Paramore (Fitzpatrick), Rachel Griffiths (Mrs Scott), Geoff Morrell (Mr Scott), Charles Bud Tingwell (Premier Berry), Saskia Burmeister (Jane Jones) 110 minutes

Story: According to the legend of Ned Kelly, the infamous bushranger, his family, the Kelly gang, robbed banks and gave the money to the poor people in Victoria who were discriminated against by the corrupt police force. The screenplay sticks to the main facts of Kelly's life but deviates with a few unnecessary Hollywood-style subplots, such as a romance with a wealthy, married woman. Jim Kelly, the only brother that survived Ned, would have been greatly offended had he been alive. His definitive comment on his brother's love life was: "My brother Ned was so devoted to his mother he had no 'girl'." [17]

Subtext: During Australia's history, the Kelly Gang story has been taught in schools and universities to remind the people of Australia that it is possible to fight against authority. It reminds Australians that they can take the law into their own hands when faced with the kind of discrimination on display here: a sister that was sexually harassed by the police, family members repeatedly jailed, beaten and harassed with no evidence, and their livelihood stolen.

Background: The acting received a great deal of acclaim with Heath Ledger cutting a very realistic Ned Kelly figure. The same height and size as Ned, he even fitted perfectly into Ned's original armoured suit. [18]

Verdict: Despite criticism that the film's screenplay deviates from facts it must be remembered that it is based on a legend. 3/5

Japanese Story (2003)

Directed by: Sue Brooks

Written by: Alison Tilson

Produced by: Davis Lightfoot, Sue Maslin, Magnus Mansie

Edited by: Jill Bilcock

Cinematography: Ian Baker

Cast: Toni Collette (Sandy Edwards), Gotaro Tsunashima (Tachibana Hiromitsu), Matthew Dykynski (Bill Baird), Lynette Curran (Mum), Yumiko Tanaka (Yukiko Hiromitsu), Kate Atkinson (Jackie), Bill Young (Jimmie Smithers) 110 minutes

Story: Two unlikely companions take a dangerous journey through the Australian desert (or dessert as Tachibana calls it). Sandy Edwards is the stereotypical tom-boy, Aussie woman and Tachibana is the stereotypical up-tight, Japanese business-man who can't allow himself to lose face to a woman or accept safety advice from her.

This is about the dangers of false pride, dealing as it does with the problem of Japanese multi-national companies coming into Australia and buying mines out in the middle of the desert. Without knowing the first thing about the Australian outback, they lack the ability to humble themselves in order to seek advice. The younger generation of Japan has similar problems with the traditional cultures of Japan, and many contemporary Japanese films deal with these issues of tradition and losing face.

Eventually the businessman's exaltation of his own race and his lack of knowledge about the natural environment has deadly results.

Subtext: The Australian environment has almost always been underestimated by foreigners looking to settle, buy or even holiday here. It is an empty country and instead of doing battle with other people for survival you do battle with the elements. It is a lesson for both cultures. Australians must not sacrifice their integrity and land because of their greed for foreign money, and strangers must learn to respect the culture and soil.

Background: At the Cannes film festival alone, Japanese Story won Best Film, Best Director, Best Actress, Best Cinematography and Best Composer. The cinematography of acclaimed Ian Baker is visually beautiful.

Verdict: I have mentioned Baker's flair for capturing the Australian environment in previous chapters but coupled here with outstanding direction by Sue Brooks and, as always, a brilliant performance by Toni Collette, it makes for an Australian film classic. 5/5

Gettin' Square (2003)

Directed by: John Teplitzky

Written by: Chris Nyst

Produced by: Trish Lake, Martin Fabinyi, Timothy White, Chris Nyst

Edited by: Ken Sallows

Cinematography: Garry Phillips

Cast: Sam Worthington (Barry Wirth), David Wenham (Johnny Spitieri), Timothy Spall (Darren Barrington), Freya

Stafford (Annie Flynn), Gary Sweet (Chicka Martin), David Roberts (Niall Toole), David Field (Arnie DeViers), Luke Pegler (Joey Wirth), Richard Carter (Craig 'Crusher' Knobes), Mitchell Butel (Con Katsakis), Garry Waddell (Dennis Obst), John Brumpton (Lenny Morrison), Helen Thomson (Marion Barrington), Marea Lambert Barker (Cheryl), Joe Bugner (Big Mick), Ugly Dave Gray (Jack Cullan), Steven Tandy (Warren Halliwell), Jonathan Biggins (Richard Dent QC), Carol Burns (Parole Board Chairman) 100 minutes

Story: Barry and Johnny Spits are fresh out of prison and are intent on gettin' square, in other words staying on the right side of the law. Their old crime boss Chicka has different plans. Events are complicated when they discover that the crooked police as well as the money hungry tax investigators are all out for their blood, or money.

Subtext: Johnny Spits is a classic idiot savant, but the Australian yobo version. He sports a mullet which is a genuine relic of the 80s and on the odd occasion he is seen being chased down the street by cops in his y-front undies and rubber thongs.

At the climax of the film a bunch of fancy lawyers and a QC try to trick Spits into squealing on a criminal mate but he runs rings around them all with complaints that no one has paid for his return bus fare from the court house and that he is going to be late to pick up his methadone.

His crowning moment of genius, however, is when he fakes his own death during a robbery, fooling the tax investigators, the federal police and the Gold Coast crime bosses, as well as making away with $400,000 in cash.

Background: Johnny Spits is played by David Wenham, famous for his roles in films such as *The Lord of the Rings*, *Sea Change* (Diver Dan), *Cosi* and *Idiot Box*.

The author, Christ Nyst, is something of a celebrity criminal lawyer in Australia. He writes crime novels based on his experiences and has defended famous criminals and politicians. *Gettin' Square* is set and filmed in his home town, The Gold Coast, which is a popular destination for tourists.

The film is a testament to the boom Australian cinema has had over the past few decades, with most of the crew having an extensive and impressive filmography of work on prior pioneering films. For example, cinematographer Garry Phillips had worked previously on some brilliant productions, including *Caddie* and *Young Einstein* as well as *Dark City*. The art director, Jenny O'Connell, started in the 90s with films such as *Street Fighter*, *The Thin Red Line* and *Oscar and Lucinda*, and then went on to work on films such as *Moulin Rouge* and *Nugget*.

Verdict: Chris Nyst's humorous, tight scripting is only now beginning to be appreciated by audiences and readers. *Gettin' Square* won a few awards but there is surely more fame in store for this Gold Coast lawyer. 5/5

Somersault (2004)

Directed by: Cate Shortland

Written by: Cate Shortland

Produced by: Anthony Anderson, Jan Chapman

Edited by: Scott Gray

Cinematography: Robert Humphreys

Cast: Abbie Cornish (Heidi), Sam Worthington (Joe), Lynette Curran (Irene), Erik Thomson (Richard), Hollie Andrew

(Bianca), Leah Purcell (Diane), Olivia Pigeot (Nicole), Blake Pittman (Karl) 106 minutes

Story: The psyche and characterisation of teenage runaway, Heidi, played by Abbie Cornish, is extremely original. On the surface she is exceptionally attractive but underneath, emotionally broken. Her good looks give her body and her sexuality a value and she confuses sexual abuse and desire of her body with love. She finds herself drawn to men as they give her affection and isolated from women because they see her as a threat. She is treated mostly as a physical entity rather than an emotional one, especially by her 'boyfriend' who is the stereotypical silent, unemotional Aussie man. Heidi is confused by her hunger for love and affection and what she is fed; offers of sex.

Subtext: Set near Jindabyne, the isolation of the landscape supports Heidi's isolation. She is separated and attacked by society for her strong and youthful feminine sexuality.

Background: Young Aussie actor Sam Worthington seems to be typecast as this cold-hearted, hard-working, slightly cruel Australian man; it would be interesting to see him branch out in future roles.

The camera work and cinematography have been highly acclaimed, complete with atmospheric blue tones and the symbolic red knitted glove reminiscent of the little red coated girl in *Schindler's List*. The film also invokes the squashed female spirit in Sylvia Plath's poem *Daddy*.

Verdict: These blue toned artistic sequences sometimes appear contrived, especially when contrasted with the gritty bedroom and shower scenes. The film is professionally shot though, and does revolve around very original characterisation. While the absence of dialogue and plot are an attempt at symbolism, this only serves to drag the film out and it does become boring towards the end. Also unsettling is the requisite inclusion of the naked pubescent girl, which seemed to sit well with a lot of reviewers. The film won all thirteen awards at AFI and was selected at the Cannes Film Festival. 3.5/5

Oyster Farmer (2005)

Directed by: Anna Reeves

Written by: Anna Reeves

Produced by: Robert Bevan, Mikael Borglund, Anthony Buckley, Keith Hayley, Hilary Davis, Andrew Mackie, Sue MacKay, Stephen Margolis, Cyril Megret, Richard Peyton, Charlie Savill, Emile Sherman, Jonathan Shteinman, Piers Tempest

Edited by: Peter Beston, Jamie Trevill

Cinematography: Alun Bollinger

Cast: Kerry Armstrong (Trish), Alan Cinis (Slug), David Field (Brownie), Diana Glenn (Pearl), Claudia Harrison (Nikki), Brady Kitchingham (Heath), Paul J. Mailath (Farmer), Jim Norton (Mumbles), Alex O'Lachlan (Jack), Jack Thompson (Skippy), Bob Yearly (Bruce) 91 minutes

Story: Jack, the oyster farmer, invents an ingenious way to steal some money for his sister, Nikki, who he injured in a car accident. Using an edible weapon (a lobster) and face mask (a fruit roll-up), he robs an armoured van, posts the money to himself and then eats the evidence.

As luck would have it the mailman dies of a heart attack and the mail is stolen (including Jack's ill-acquired fortune).

The mystery and the characters that surround Jack's search for the cash merge as a multitude of possibilities surface.

Soon the hunt for the money retreats and the hunt for life becomes more important. It becomes apparent that the oyster farmers living on the Hawkesbury River don't need lots of cash and flashy boats. They are happy to just live and love and eat lots of fresh seafood.

When the mystery is finally solved it is not, surprisingly, the climax of the movie. Instead the climax is the characters' final understanding of themselves and the nature of love.

Subtext: The love stories between main characters Pearl and Jack and between Trish and Brownie are punctuated by photography so poignant that it should be hanging in an art gallery.

It was wonderful that the characters came to the realisation that the stolen money was useless for improving their quality of life. Although the film contained drama, it was not dramatic because the characters were all forgiving of each other's mistakes, resulting in a meditative, peaceful film.

Background: "Wakey Wakey, hand off snaky": This is a true Australian film. The river landscapes, shot wonderfully by cinematographer Alun Bollinger, provide the perfect backdrop for the down-to-earth realism of the script. The design of the film is gritty yet clean and it captures the Australian working spirit in all its varied temperatures.

Verdict: If only the film could have been longer so we could have seen even more of the interesting characters, such as Skippy (Jack Thomson). This is Anna Reeves first film and hopefully there will be many more to come. 5/5

Peaches (2005)

Directed by: Craig Monahan

Written by: Sue Smith

Produced by: Judith McCann, Margot McDonald, Craig Monahan, Don Reynolds, Nicolas Stiliadis, Roslyn Walker

Edited by: Suresh Ayyar

Cinematography: Ernie Clark

Cast: Hugo Weaving (Alan), Jacqueline McKenzie (Jude), Emma Lung (Steph), Tyson Contor (Johnny), Sam Healy (Jass), Matthew Le Nevez (Brian)

Story: Alan, a union activist with a stutter, leaves the love of his life, Jude, when she has trouble coping with her sister's sudden death. Alan can't handle Jude in mourning, nor can he cope with the new child that Jude has adopted (her dead sister's child). 18 years later the child is a young woman, Steph. A seduction occurs and Alan has a sexual relationship with the girl who should have been his daughter. He also betrays the union members of the peach factory where the whole town works, and helps to have it shut down, leaving everyone without a job.

Subtext: It is a complex story that deserves credit for its realism and depth of character but it is let down by the resolution. Jude is blamed for Steph's sheltered up-bringing and Steph leaves for the sunny skies of Queensland with an ex-convict who is Alan's half-brother. Meanwhile the incestuous Alan is welcomed back into Jude's life with no fuss. Alan's wife and three kids never appear on screen. Alan's behaviour thus seems vindicated whereas Jude has been admonished for raising her dead sister's child.

Background: This is another sterling performance from Hugo Weaving, matched by the talented Jacqueline McKenzie (*Romper Stomper, Mr Reliable*) and newcomer Emma Lung.

Verdict: Watch it for the awe-inspiring photography, detailed character performances and complex screenplay. There is also a great quip about hitch-hiker murders (see *Wolf Creek*). 3/5

Wolf Creek (2005)

Directed by: Greg McLean

Written by: Greg McLean

Produced by: George Adams, Martin Fabinyi, Michael Gudinski, Gary Hamilton, Matt Hearn, Simon Hewitt, David Lightfoot, Greg McLean

Edited by: Jason Ballantine

Cast: John Jarratt (Mick Taylor), Cassandra Magrath (Liz Hunter), Andy McPhee (Bazza), Kestie Morassi (Kristy Earl), Guy Petersen (Swedish Backpacker 1), Nathan Phillips (Ben Mitchell), Gordon Poole (Attendant), Jenny Starwall (Swedish Backpacker #2), Aaron Sterns (Bazza's Mate) 95 minutes

Story: Three backpackers are abducted in South Australia and two are gruesomely and graphically murdered. This horror film is not for the faint hearted. John Jarratt, who has starred in many great Australian films including *We of the Never Never*, *The Chant of Jimmie Blacksmith* and *Picnic at Hanging Rock*, plays the convincingly friendly Aussie with sinister undertones.

Subtext: This is based on true incidents of murders that have been committed in Australia.

Background: The most successful Australian film to date even prior to being released into cinemas. It was bought by Miramax for $7.5 million and was made for $1.4 million[19].

Verdict: Shown at the Cannes Film Festival in 2005. This is truly horrifying and disturbing, combining the excellent realism of Australian cinema with terrifying landscapes.

Afterword:
Australian Cinema, The Traditions

The Australian film industry has one advantage over similar industries in other countries, namely the Australian Film Finance Corporation. There is still little money in movies in Australia, unlike Hollywood, where it is big business, and as a result, most films are financed by this fund. The result is an industry that reflects the socialist spirit (tempered with more than a little harmless government propaganda) of the nation.

To secure film finance in Australia typical Hollywood studio product – silicon implants, car chases and petrol tanker explosions – won't help. The film finance corporation has a history of helping directors who portray Australian character, ideals, history, classic literature, innovation and integrity. If it sounds like a recipe for a propaganda machine, it isn't really all that bad.

Australian cinema did indeed begin as a propaganda tool: the government used film in the late 1800s, not to make feature productions, but to entice migrants to the empty colony. Now, Australians have a great reputation for their honesty, friendliness and down to earth self consciousness. Why? Because that's how our film industry advertises us. As Bruce Beresford said, "The Australian Prime Minister should be kissing the bums of the filmmakers."[20]

The film industry has actually done a great job of recording the country's history and staying true to the Aussie ideals as a result of funding. More needs to be done, however, to protect

Australian content from being wiped out by the commercial distribution machine. While distribution has proved a hindrance by pandering to Hollywood, the Australian Education Department has been a big help, teaching Australian film to the general population. The film school NIDA has also produced the majority of the country's internationally famous film stars and crews, with Mel Gibson contributing heavily to its funding and creating a good example for other Australian stars to follow.

If you study Australian film from beginning to end you are studying the history of Australia because it is a young country which has the advantage of having had the use of film to document the majority of its brief history. From the birth of the nation, recorded in the world's first documentary, through the decades of social, environmental and political change we can watch the development of the Australian character and culture as viewed through the eyes of artists.

One thing is very clear from the history lesson they've left us with: if you work hard with a smile on your face and you manage to stoush a copper at least once in your lifetime then you must be a good sort no matter if you're a 'pom', 'black-fella', 'tart', 'bloke', 'wog', 'kiwi', 'yobo' or any other type of 'bloody Aussie'.

Notes

1. ABC, 2001, *The Story of The Kelly Gang*, Australian Broadcasting Corporation (online), available at http://www.abc.net.au/limelight/docs/films/5_1_2_4.htm

2. Bagnall, Frank, *The Pictures That Moved* (video recording), 1964, Film Australia.

3. Penrose, H, Pertzel, B, Walters, F, Waterhouse, C, 2005, *History Smiths*, HistorySmiths Pty Ltd, (online) available at- http://www.historysmiths.com.au

4. *The Princess Bride* (video recording) 1987, USA, Magna Pacific.

5. Gow, Keith, *Now You're Talking 1930–1940*, (video recording) 1979, Film Australia.

6. Gow, Keith, *Now You're Talking 1930–1940*, (video recording) 1979, Film Australia.

7. Gow, Keith, *Now You're Talking 1930–1940*, (video recording) 1979, Film Australia.

8. ABC, 2004, *Famous Australians* Australian Broadcasting Corporation (online) available at http://www.abc.net.au/btn/australians/cksmith.htm

9. Francis, Robert, *The Celluloid Heroes: 1896–1996, Celebrating 100 years of Australian Cinema* (video recording DVD) 1995, Film Australia.

10. Francis, Robert, *The Celluloid Heroes: 1896–1996, Celebrating 100 years of Australian Cinema* (video recording DVD) 1995, Film Australia.

11. Francis, Robert, *The Celluloid Heroes: 1896–1996, Celebrating 100 years of Australian Cinema* (video recording

DVD) 1995, Film Australia.

12. IMDB *Walkabout*, 2005, Internet Movie Database, Seattle, available at http://www.imdb.com/

13. Francis, Robert, *The Celluloid Heroes: 1896–1996, Celebrating 100 years of Australian Cinema* (video recording DVD) 1995, Film Australia.

14. Francis, Robert, *The Celluloid Heroes: 1896–1996, Celebrating 100 years of Australian Cinema* (video recording DVD) 1995, Film Australia.

15. Thompson, H.S. *Hell's Angels*, 1996, Ballantine Books, New York.

16. Francis, Robert, *The Celluloid Heroes: 1896–1996, Celebrating 100 years of Australian Cinema* (video recording DVD) 1995, Film Australia.

17. IMDB *Ned Kelly*, 2005, Internet Movie Database, Seattle, available at http://www.imdb.com/

18. IMDB *Ned Kelly*, 2005, Internet Movie Database, Seattle, available at http://www.imdb.com/

19. Kalina, P, *Dream Run For Local Horror Film*, (online) The Age, April 27, 2005, available at http://www.theage.com.au/articles/2003/03/28/1048653852118.html?oneclick=true

20. Francis, Robert, *The Celluloid Heroes: 1896–1996, Celebrating 100 years of Australian Cinema* (video recording DVD) 1995, Film Australia.

Index

INDEX